Becoming Auma

a novel
inspired by true events

melinda josiah geaumont

ISBN: 1-4196-7456-0

ISBN-13: 978-1419674563

Visit www.booksurge.com to order additional copies.

For Aaron and Caitlin

Acknowledgments

I would like to personally thank all the people who believed in me, even when I didn't believe in myself. For his patience and encouragement always, love and gratitude to my husband Jeff. A heartfelt thank you to all my family, for you continue to inspire me. Special thanks goes out to my dear friends Diane Ames, editor extraordinaire, and Selena Brock for her photographic expertise! Thanks to all my early readers Patty Paradis, Rita McGrath, Melody Wood, Jody Jansen, JoAnne Wilson, Evelyn Labree, Caitlin Madison, Rachel Wilson, Amanda Josiah Page, Amy Shannon and Laura Josiah for their support and insight along the way. And lastly, a toast, to the women for whom this story was written - Jo, Sue, Teri, Patty, Debi, Diane, Kelly, Sharon, Mary, Vickie, Beth, Selena and Becky for all the laughter you've brought to my life!

❦

Why is it that there are never any Kleenex when you need them? As Emma dabbed her eyes with a ball of wadded up toilet paper, she glanced in the mirror. "I look a bit like her," she thought. "I have her smile." Emma's wide smile was never a favorite feature. Perhaps her upper gum showed a little too much and the smile was a bit crooked, but on this day, sharing a smile seemed like such a special thing. It was as though Emma could feel her presence, as though it was she who was smiling back. As Emma kicked off her shoes and slipped slowly out of her black dress, she sat on the edge of her queen size mahogany bed and began to cry again. "This too shall pass." The words and phrases swirled in her head as she replayed the stories shared with her through the years and over the past two months. She looked at the pile of journals and notebooks sitting on the desk and wondered if, when she herself was old, she too would have a legacy to pass down. Emma doubted that her own lifetime would hold as many close calls, adventures or lifelong friendships. "I suppose that is what made her so wonderful," thought Emma as she tossed the sodden ball of toilet paper into the trash can. Memories good and bad tell our life's story. But memories are nothing without people to share them with.

The church was packed with people. Here to pay tribute were family members and friends who had known her over the years, but many of her closest friends were already gone. After all, she had turned 84 this past April and that would have made some of them, had they been living, over 90. Emma had learned that two now lived with their families in other states and one was sadly in a nursing home. As Emma walked slowly down the aisle and looked around the room, she saw her Uncle Adam sitting with his family in the first pew. Next to him sat Grampie. He looked so lost without her. Emma's 11-year-old son Glenn made his way toward his great grandfather and gave him a big hug. Grampie always loved kids and having Glenn to talk to was a nice diversion. Emma smiled at her parents, John and Elizabeth, seated in the next pew, and was glad to see that her mom was being supported by her dad's strong arm around her shoulders. Aunt Elaine sat on Elizabeth's right giving comfort to her best friend. "I don't know how she is holding up so well," thought Emma as she reflected on how she would feel given the same circumstance. She sat down next to Grampie and put her arm around him. As Emma turned to look into the sea of people, she gave a wave to her great aunts and their clan who sat huddled together one pew back. They had all come to remember her. Both aunts were quite elderly now; 77 and 80 respectively. They were her sisters and their grief weighed heavily about them. The three of them had always been very close. Losing a sister is like losing a part of one's self.

She had touched many lives. But as the myriad of people came through the line, it was the three old women huddled together, wearing oversized fur coats, that caught Emma's eye. They seemed to be looking past the friend who lay lifeless before them, focusing instead on the collection of pictures arranged on the photo displays. Pictures that they knew too well. While Emma knew some of the original group by name, she knew all of them by reputation. These were the remnants of the group of women once called "The Society". Their lifelong friendship had sculpted her character and, in essence, had created the woman Emma affectionately called "Auma".

One might think that she would have been called Grandma or Grammie or even Nana, but that was too conventional for her group of friends. They had decided long ago that come the day they were to be grandmothers, each would be called "Auma" - because of all the "drama and trauma" of raising their own kids. Their friendship gave new meaning to every aspect of their adult lives, and when one of them did something, they all did something. They shared the ups and downs, the good and the bad, the laughter and the tears. From one seemingly insignificant conversation grew many of the schemes and adventures that made their lives worth talking about. And over the years, Auma had become a master of taking the ball and running with it. This is her story.

◦◦◦

Chapter One
Before She Was Auma

August 17, 2047

As I sit here sipping my morning cup of coffee, I feel so blessed to enjoy this day. The sun is shining, the birds are chirping and a warm breeze blows across the porch as I write. What a marvelous day to be alive! Every day should be enjoyed in this way! Today is Emma's 35th birthday and I've been thinking about something special that I'd like to share with her this year. When Elizabeth gave me this book for my birthday, I was reminded of how much I used to write. I dug through my closet to pull out all my old journals. It seems that I might be missing a few, but it's hard to remember for sure. Years ago I was so good at writing down my thoughts and after reading through a few of them, I've decided to give my journals to Emma. Perhaps she will appreciate getting to know her grandmother a bit better. This is such a hard time for her with her divorce from Nick and trying to take care of Glenn. I can remember a time in my own life when I felt a bit that way, and maybe knowing that will give her a new understanding of things. Life's journey has its ups and downs, but ultimately it is up to us to make the most of every moment and learn along the way. I look back myself and thank God for all of it. It really has been a wonderful life.

Settling in with a steaming cup of hot cocoa, Emma sat cross-legged on the floor of her bedroom. Spread out across the carpet were the old books and photo albums. Just a month and a half before Emma had celebrated her 35th birthday. So much had happened since then. . . in some families, birthdays come and go without much fanfare, but when you were related to Auma, every birthday was one worth celebrating. The family would come together to have dinner and eat the birthday person's favorite cake, ending the evening with an out of tune "Happy Birthday to you". Even if you were away, Auma would make a point to call and sing you a birthday greeting on your cell and send you a card with $50. It didn't matter how old you were, or how old she was, she always remembered. This birthday had been somewhat different though. It was the first year after Emma's divorce from Nick, and Auma knew how difficult it was for her. They had planned to do the family birthday thing, but Auma insisted on also going out to dinner, "just the two of them".

As they sat together at a cozy booth in Jerry's Diner, Auma held Emma's hands across the table. "I'm 84 this year, you know, and I think that it's time for you to have these," she said. "After all, the Shaman told me long ago that this would be my year." Emma wasn't really sure what she meant by that, but watched her grandmother curiously. Carefully, Auma put a box on the table. It was wrapped in shiny paper, but not elaborately, as she was never all about wrapping. It was what was inside that mattered - a sentiment Auma held to be true not only for gifts but also in life. "This, my dear, is my gift to you. Right now, you feel alone and scared. You wonder where your life will take you and who you will become. You are a single mom and want to do the best for your child. I once felt that way. I was not always the woman you've come to know. Not all memories are good ones. We have times in our lives when difficult or unexpected things happen, but it is what we do with them that matters. Challenges allow us to grow and bring us to new paths along life's journey. Find happiness within yourself, for if you are not happy with who you are, you will never be happy in a relationship. Take the time to build friendships - the women you call friends can be your lifeline. Don't be afraid to take chances because the times you take risks often lead to new and wonderful adventures. And lastly, love life! Love it for all that its worth and make the most of every single moment, one day at a time." As Auma gave her little speech, Emma carefully opened the box to find over a dozen books. There were clothbound journals, little girl diaries with tiny locks, spiral notebooks of different shapes and sizes, and two old fashioned photo albums. With tears in her blue faded eyes, Auma said, "Happy 35th Birthday, Emma! I give you the story of my life".

As the next week passed, Emma began to read through Auma's journals with a growing curiosity to know who her grandmother really was. She knew Auma as the family matriarch. Her strength and insight remained strong in spite of her age and she always carried herself as a woman with purpose. People often said that Auma made things happen and, in thinking back on her own life, Emma knew this to be true. Her grandmother brought life to every situation and could raise people up just by being around. She was humble about the effect she had on people, as though it was no big deal, but her love reached out to make a difference in people's lives. Emma wondered if Auma had always been this way or if she'd come to this over the course of her lifetime. She asked herself how she could learn to hold that positive energy, too. Perhaps that was what Auma wanted her to discover. By giving her the journals, Emma knew it was Auma's way of "planting a seed" and encouraging her to be mindful of what is most important in life.

She called Auma one afternoon in early September with an invitation to lunch on Saturday in the hope that her grandmother might shed more light on her life's story in her own words. There were so many things Emma hoped to learn. When Saturday came, she drove Glenn over to his dad's house for his weekend visitation and then waited patiently for Auma to arrive. Emma glanced down at the books that lay scattered on her living room coffee table. Auma was a prolific writer who at times had written pages and pages of random thoughts and introspection along the way. But then, unexpectedly, months and even years had passed with no more than a few words or a lone paragraph being written. Fortunately, it seemed that eventually time would drive her forward once again to pick up her preferred blue pen. It wasn't that Auma's life was exceptional. She was not famous and she didn't do anything overly extraordinary, but perhaps that is what made her story worth sharing. Her ordinary life beckoned. Like many of us, she seemed to start out a bit unsure of herself, but her lifelong determination was remarkable. "Who really is this woman I call Auma?" thought Emma.

A small yellow child's diary first stood out among the pile. On the cover the words "My Diary" were printed in gold ink under a picture of a little old fashioned girl in a pinafore and bonnet. As Emma opened the book she saw the uneven sprawl of a child's handwriting written in blue ink:

July 4, 1976

Dear Diary,

Well today was the Big Day! July 4th 1976! The big Bicentennial. There was a parade in town and I worked in Daddy's shop today. Mom and Dad gave me 25 cents an hour. I made $2.25! All day I wore a bicentennial costume. I had short pants like knickers and a white shirt that buttoned up the front and a black tri-cornered hat. We sell those hats in the store. I know it's a boy's costume, but I don't care. Susan and Beth wore girl costumes with dresses and aprons and little white bonnets, but I hate that girly stuff. I'm a tomboy! It is cool to be a tomboy. Daddy's shop has penny candy and lots of kids came in today to buy some. The store is a neat place. Daddy has lots of antiques and "Early American Gift Accessories" – at least that is what the sign says. It smells good, like cinnamon and pine, and I sit behind the counter by the big red coffee grinder. I feel grown up when I work there, like I'm in charge. Today was a good day. I think we made $100. That was pretty good. I think Dad was happy. I hope I made him proud.

Tonight we went to the Nottingham fireworks, but it was not good cause kids were throwing firecrackers and it was dangerous. We ate cotton candy though and Daddy won Beth a stuffed animal. Mom and Dad's anniversary is coming up and we are going to take them to Kentucky Fried Chicken. I think I'll have saved enough to treat. I'm supposed to babysit for Marianne next week, too, and so I might make another $2.

It's late and I should go to sleep.

Bye for now.

Emma flipped a little ahead and read –

September 1, 1976

This is the first diary I have kept for a long time. It tells of my day to day life in the bicentennial year. It's a good year to keep a diary. I turned 13 in April and that is a big deal. I'm officially a teenager! I am going into the 8th grade next week. I can't wait because my class will finally be the oldest ones in Northwood Elementary. We got to order new school clothes from the Sears Catalogue. I picked out new brown Levi corduroys and a plaid shirt. It has gold thread that goes through it and I think it looks cool. Daddy let Susan and Beth pick stuff too. Beth starts first grade this year. I like school and I'm pretty smart, but I wish I was prettier. I have always been the "chubby" one in my family. People say that and I hate it. The boys at school say mean things too sometimes, like "candy lover" because of the store, but I don't really eat candy a lot. Mom and Dad don't let us. My hair is brown and straight and kinda long. I used to want to look like Marcia Brady, but I'm not as thin. I'm getting taller – almost 5'7" but I weigh 125 pounds. Maybe I am fat. I don't have my period yet. Sometimes I think that there is something wrong with me. Lots of my friends have it already. I read <u>Are You There God, It's Me Margaret</u> this summer – I love that book – and my favorite shows are "The Waltons" and "The Six Million Dollar Man". Steve Austin is a cool guy. I wish I had bionics. Then I'd be good at gym. By the way. . ... don't tell anyone. I have a boyfriend! Maybe I'll put his picture in here so that you can see. And some love notes. He writes me nice notes. I think I love Richie. He's a little younger than me, but I don't care. He is the first boy I have kissed. I mean on the lips. Joe didn't count in 6th grade. Richie wore a tiny bit of his sister's Lip Smacker lip-gloss – Strawberry Flavor so it would taste good.

It's late and I'm supposed to be asleep, so I better go. Remember me as 13 – a simple young teenager in NH.

P.S. Sorry if that sounds corny.

Bye for now.

Smiling to herself, Emma ran her hands over the page. Flipping to the back of the book she noticed an old yellowed school picture and a tarnished gold plated ring with the letter "R". Auma was smiling her same crooked smile into the camera. How is it that our experiences shape the people we become, and how did this self-conscious little girl become my tenacious grandmother? Emma wondered. Her curiousity grew. As she thumbed through the books in front of her, she put them in order by date and found a spiral notebook that seemed the next in line. Teenage bubble writing with large dotted I's and many exclamations jumped from the pages. She read on.

April 7, 1979

We celebrated my birthday yesterday! I'm turning 16 on the 12th! Sweet Sixteen, but I have been kissed! Whoever made up that dumb saying didn't know anything. I don't know any 16 year olds who haven't been kissed at least once. Maybe in the olden days or something. My birthday was kind of good and kind of bad. It started out good, cause I had 8 of my friends from school over for my slumber party and we went to Pizza Hut in Newington. But then, after we all ate, they had the stupid waitress come over and sing "Happy Birthday" to me in front of the whole dumb restaurant! I almost died!!! Why would they do that to me?!! I ran out of the restaurant and sat in the station wagon. Mom came out and tried to get me to come back in, but I wouldn't go. I guess that was dumb on my part, but I couldn't face those people! Finally we left the restaurant and went to the movies. I got myself in a better mood and we saw the movie "China Syndrome". It was good and we liked it. After the movie, we went back home and we all had cake and I opened presents. I'm starting up a hope chest and collecting stuff so that someday I can have my own apartment or house. That was what I wanted this birthday and so that was what everyone got me. I got a brown cookie jar and some kitchen towels and a container with wooden spoons and stuff. I also got an Anne Murray album. Susan and Beth gave me a new blue nightshirt. Mom and Dad gave me a charm bracelet and a little matchbox car. They thought that was funny! I'm about to get my license, but I knew they wouldn't get me a real car. They don't have the money. I was hoping that I might get a stereo, though. That was what I really wanted, so I was disappointed. The charm bracelet didn't do much for me. I shouldn't be ungrateful. Mom and Dad try really hard. I always expect too much. Why do I do that?!

Then after presents, me and all my friends camped out on the living room floor in sleeping bags. They were all fighting over who would sleep next to who and no one seemed to care about being next to me! It's my birthday! I'm the one they should want to be next to! They were all laughing and eating cheese curls and M&M's and didn't even notice that I wasn't there. I was in the bathroom crying. Sometimes I am an idiot!

Day to day accounts of going to school or the mall mingled with stories of babysitting and family events. And then, without warning, the writing stopped. At least for a while. In 1981 how old would Auma have been? Around 18 or so. Such a long, long time ago. Inside the brown leather journal, the handwriting became more precise and linear, as though its author had made a conscious effort to be artistic. By sharing her journals and her deepest thoughts, Auma was encouraging Emma to get to know her true self. Already, this was becoming Emma's own personal journey.

August 17, 1981

Although I've kept diaries in the past, I must admit that I've never been very good at keeping up with them. I decided that this year I would try to write down as many important events or ideas that may come to my mind. To begin, I suppose I should tell something about myself . . .

I was born on the 12th day of April in the year 1963. The year that President Kennedy was shot. I was just a baby, though, so I don't remember. Supposedly the 60's were years of chaos and craziness, but whether that's true or not I can't honestly say, but I do know it was a time of change. I was born in the decade of peace signs, happy faces, flower children and stupid words like "groovy". What a beginning, huh? By the way, my name is Laura.

I have two sisters – Susan who was born in '67 and Beth who was born in '70. They're both really sweet and fortunately, I get along with them both. Mom and Dad are great, too. . . not that we never disagree, because we do. But, for the most part we get along.

Right now I'm 18. "Legal" (whatever that means – I can't drink legally yet, as the drinking age is 21, not that I don't now and then). I graduated from Coe Brown Northwood Academy this past June and now I'm working for Nike (sneakers, not missiles) and making $7 an hour. I work in the "futures department" doing secretarial work and keeping track of orders to be shipped in the future month. I guess that is why they call it "futures". I like my job very much (and I'm lucky to have this job as work is hard to come by). The people are great and the work itself is pretty good, too. People all thought I was stupid for not going to college. I graduated as Salutatorian of my class, but I just can't see the point. I don't really know what I want to do, and Mom and Dad don't have the money to send me. Besides, I want to move on with my life. Find the right guy, get married and live on my own. I'm going out with this guy named Kevin. Kev is 17 (he's a senior this year) and he lives in Nottingham. I really like him and I've been seeing him for about 8 months now. I have my doubts about his being "Mr. Right", but time will tell. Lately things seem to be getting better between us. However, since this

*book doesn't have a lock, I won't write anything that could get
me into trouble should it be found and read. I won't lie though.
I'm still a virgin. Not that I wouldn't do it with the right guy,
but I don't want to get pregnant.*

*Although I realize that it's terrible to live on junk food, I
personally am addicted to soda – my favorite being Diet Pepsi. I
don't eat any green vegetables and I hate eggs. I guess my eating
habits aren't the best, but this is the age of fast food and I guess
I'm a product of my environment. I listen to WCOZ—94 FM
all the time and I love Sting who is the lead singer in the band,
The Police. Their new song "Don't Stand So Close To Me" is
awesome and I love "Message in a Bottle", too. Since Northwood
NH isn't exactly the most exciting place in the world to live, my
friends and I go to Concord or Newington to see movies, go to
the drive-in, or to play Space Invaders at the Dream Machine.
Besides movies and parties and being with my friends, there's
not too much I can say about my life. Some of my friends smoke
pot, but I'm not really into that. One time a few weeks back, I
was actually gonna try it, but when we went to get my friend's
weed, it had been stolen from her car. I figured it was God's way
of protecting me. Although I'm not the perfect "Christian", I do
love God and hope that my life will straighten out. I want to do
the right thing, but I'm not always sure what the right thing is.*

*It's getting late and I have to work tomorrow, so I will go,
but don't worry (I'm sure you are not), I'll be back.*

August 23, 1981

*Dad has been moody lately. He might be losing his job at the
furniture store. I know it's hard on him. I should explain about
Dad. See, he means well and I love him a lot, but I sometimes
have a tough time talking to him because he's pretty set in his ways
(most of which are what one might call "old fashioned"). I know
that he's just trying to protect me, but sometimes I don't want to
be protected. I want to be independent. I'm not a baby anymore.
Not that Dad doesn't try to be fair, because he does – it's just that*

it's hard for him to understand that things aren't the way they used to be. He hates my music and doesn't like my ripped jeans. He doesn't like that I say "yeah" instead of "yes" and he says I'm opinionated. And he isn't overjoyed about Kevin. It's just that Kevin isn't real talkative around older people and so he doesn't come down to the house as much as Dad thinks he should. Also, there was this time last year when Kevin, Scott and I stopped at the Ridge Store on our way to school and stupid Scott got caught stealing wine. I had no idea that stupid Scott did this. I was just sitting there in the truck, but none the less, when I told Dad he was not happy. I don't blame him, I guess. But it wasn't really Kevin's fault. It was Scott's. I am thinking of breaking up with Kevin though. He never calls and is always out with his friends. They are always doing stupid things and I know better. I need to get my head together. Sometimes it's hard to make everyone happy.

It seemed hard to believe that Auma could have once been so young. Youth is a difficult time for most people, filled with uncertainty. "It was for me, too," Emma thought. "I don't know how my mom put up with me some of the time. When we are teenagers we long to be grown up and when we become grown up, we long to have the freedom of teenagers."

October 31, 1981

Believe it or not it's 12:14am (November 1st actually I guess) and Halloween is over. Halloween was the <u>best,</u> most fantastic day of my entire life! Tonight was the big night out with Chris. Susan met his family at a church convention and kind of set it up for me to go out with him. I'm speechless! He's the politest guy (he opens doors and everything! I didn't know guys like him exist!) and we've got so much in common. It was so easy to talk to him. After having a cup of coffee at his house with his parents, we went out for dinner at the Bratskeller and had great food. We both like pepperoni and onion pizza! Isn't that *weird? Then we drove to the Newington Mall to see all the little kids in Halloween costumes (I can't believe he's so sentimental about holidays, too!) Over there we played pinball at Dream Machine and then drove around Portsmouth, just cruising and talking. We went on to Rye and walked along the beach (it was so beautiful and he loves the ocean!) and from there we drove to a restaurant lounge called the Red Lion. We sat in the lounge at a small table with candlelight and the band played. We got to dance and everything. We stayed there for about an hour and I drank one Tom Collins. It was good and it wasn't like I was there to get drunk – to be honest it was the first time since the "vodka incident" that I'd drunk anything. After that we went to his house and watched the end of a horror movie on HBO. All that in one night! What a great first date huh? He's so sweet! I think I'm in love already! He kisses nice, too. I can't believe that such a great guy would be interested in me. When I first met him I thought he was into disco and looked kinda like Denny Terrio from Dance Fever and I guess in a way I was right, cause he does like disco, but he's not like Denny Terrio. I don't like those Disco King guys. He does have the same hair though. He's really cute. He's thin, but not skinny, very Greek with dark hair and dark eyes and a dark mustache. He fits my description of Mr. Right. He's 5'9" so he's taller than I am, which is good, too. And he believes in God. It's like God answered my prayers.*

I better go and dream sweet dreams. . .

November 17, 1981

So much has happened, that it's hard to put it all on paper. Chris and I have seen each other every day since we first went out. I love him so much. Just being at home or at his house with him is enough as long as he is near by. I know it's only been a matter of weeks but we've been talking of marriage. He's given me roses, we've gone out to dinner, danced at clubs, gone to the movies, and spent every minute with each other. He brought me a fortune cookie that said "You will probably marry after a brief courtship" – I know it's true!

November 23, 1981

It's been six days since I've written and what a six days it has been! I'm now the proud owner of a gorgeous diamond ring. Chris and I are engaged! It's all happened so fast that I'm still in a daze. We broke the news to Mom and Dad on Friday night and although they were speechless, I know they want to be happy. Well, Mom was and Dad seemed like he was trying to be. In a way, I think Dad feels like he's losing his little girl. He likes Chris a lot and is happy for us, but the realization of the whole thing is just too much for him to handle (I guess that's understandable). Mom seems overjoyed, though, and Susan and Beth are happy, too. His parents seem thrilled and everyone else is ecstatic. The wedding will be in July! The ring we picked out is a quarter carat tiffany cut diamond and we got it from Service Merchandise. It's beautiful! I'm 18 and Chris is 20 and we are meant to be together - I just know it. I realize this is a mixed up mess, everything happening so fast and all, but right now my brain is so scrambled that I can't think. I'm just too excited! I'll write more when I calm down.

As Emma flipped the pages in the rest of the journal, she realized that this was the last entry made for many, many months. She wanted to hear about the wedding and how that all worked out, but Auma kept her guessing. The middle pages of the book were empty and she wondered what this meant. Perhaps Auma was too busy preparing for her wedding and her new life to take the time to write. Then, as suddenly as the words seemed to disappear, they returned.

October 15, 1982

Autumn is here and the leaves are all turning their beautiful colors. I've always liked fall. Work at Nike is still going well, but it gets hectic because Chris has to drive me to work in the morning and then after I work, he picks me up and takes the car at night. We are making do with our VW Rabbit. We can't afford another car. He's working nights until midnight so I spend most evenings trying to cook dinners and watching HBO. I'm not a very good cook. I was trying to make meatballs the other day and realized that they didn't come out right. When I called Mom she told me that I had forgotten to add the eggs and bread crumbs! I guess I never knew that there was more to it than just rolling them in balls and frying them. Every night I make up "tv dinners" that I package for Chris. I put them in pie plates and cover them with tin foil and label them so that when I'm at work and before he goes to work he can have something to eat. I always label them with instructions too like "put in oven for 30 min. at 350 degrees" cause he doesn't really know how to cook either. I am trying my best to be a good wife. I make his lunches and iron his shirts. We spend most Saturdays at the Laundromat, but that is ok. I don't really mind. And Sundays we go to Bible studies with his family. I like having my own apartment. It's tiny, but at least it is our own. We live right across the street from Berwick Academy and nearby is a Cumberland Farms which is convenient if I need to buy milk. The only thing that is a little annoying is a very large Asian family lives down stairs and they are sometimes noisy. They cook a lot of very spicy food which makes the hallway smell weird. I think at least six people live there. I guess knowing that, I feel fortunate, because in our apartment there are only two of us.

Sometimes Chris and I fight over stupid things. He has particular ways of doing things and maybe I am less particular. He is fussy about wasting water or worrying about my breaking stuff like his stereo or scratching his albums. As if I'd break his stereo! He's kind of like that with the car, too. We got in a big fight last week and he actually threw his hairbrush at me. He has his own special hairbrush. I think that's dumb. I told him

I'll leave him if he does it again, but I didn't really mean it. I do love him.

I've been thinking a lot about having a baby. I can't see why we should wait. I know I would make a good mother and Chris would be a good dad. We want to have kids and I am almost 20. I don't want to be an old mother. I want to have fun with my kids.

Again time moved ahead and there were few entries. How young Auma was back then! Being 20 is the time in your life when you desperately want to feel like a grown up and live your life as your own, and yet in retrospect, most of us look back and realize just how young we really were at 20. Emma thought of herself at that age, halfway through college and head over heels in love with Nick. Independence and carving out a life of your own is what being 20 is all about. As the pages continued, Auma wrote a few short passages about work and what they ate for dinner, but then nothing again for a while. Perhaps that was why she took a hiatus at times. There was nothing of great importance to say.

September 25, 1983

I am in the last sessions of my Lamaze class and I am so thankful that Mom can go with me. Chris is working nights and unable to attend them and so Mom is going to be my coach when I deliver the baby. Chris will be in there, too, but Mom will be the one helping me breathe and all. I'm so huge, but I feel ok now. I was so sick in the beginning. I'm finally done with work and I think Chris and I have decided that I will try and stay home full time. We don't make a lot of money, but if I had to pay for day care it would mostly take up most of what I make. We'll just live carefully. I decorated the baby's room in our mobile home and it looks really cute. I made felt balloons in all different colors for the wall and I received many nice things at my baby shower. Plus I got tons of hand me downs from Chris' aunt. We are as prepared as we are going to be. I'm kinda scared about the delivery, though. I don't know what to expect and I can't imagine that breathing is going to make it not hurt. Sometimes I hate it when Mom and I are at the class, cause I feel like the other older couples are looking at me. Like I'm some teenage pregnant girl. My wedding ring doesn't fit anymore and so it does look that way. But I want to tell everyone that my husband is at work and I really am married. I think I'm having a boy. I don't know why, but I just really think that I am. We chose the name Adam. My due date of Oct.3rd is coming up.

Chris and I are doing pretty good. Money is tight but we are getting by. I can't wait to have our baby. I know that I will be a good mom. We both want to be good parents.

Auma arrived for lunch right on time. She always had a thing about being punctual. Uncle Adam had given her a ride over, as Auma's eyesight wasn't what it used to be and neither she nor Grampie drove anymore. Her 5'7" frame was a bit shorter then it had been when she was younger, but Auma still held her head high. In her youth, she had walked into a room with presence. She had a distinctive walk; a bit heavy in the heel and a long stride that made others take notice of her arrival. Now, her arthritis limited her mobility a bit and she moved at a slower, yet still determined, pace. Her once brown hair was mixed with gray, although not entirely silver, and was worn in a short "sassy" style. That's what Auma called it. Like her own father, she had grayed slowly over the years, but had colored it brown until a few years ago when she decided to let it go natural. The wrinkles around her eyes were deep and her laugh lines deeper, but she maintained that both were trophies from years of things to smile about. Her distinctive blue eyes had grown a bit cloudy over time, as though they held within them all the secrets of her life, but they still contained a glimmer of the sparkle that once made them her best feature. Auma was easily winded when she moved about, but living with one lung had that effect. Rather than letting this condition limit her, however, Auma focused on appreciating each breath and being mindful in her living.

That afternoon following lunch, Emma sat next to Auma on the couch. As they sipped cinnamon apple tea together, Emma began to read out loud from the books on the table. Her grandmother sat quietly and closed her eyes as if trying to remember each moment in time. Eighty-four years is a lot to recall and her memory wasn't quite what it used to be, but as Emma read, Auma's story unfolded one page, one moment, at a time. She remembered. Her voice, her youthful intonation resounded in the written words and as they read together, Auma herself began to take up where the youthful author had left off, filling in all the details of her story. Life is full of secrets and Auma always loved a good mystery. Delving into the journals was like rediscovering the map that would bring the reader to a hidden treasure. Treasure that perhaps Auma herself had buried years before. With the hint of life's secrets yet to share, Auma smiled mischievously and gave Emma a wink. Hand in hand they'd begun their journey together.

⚜

Chapter Two
Coming Together

November 17, 1990

The most wonderful thing about a girlfriend is that not only does she understand you, but she can usually be counted on to cheer you up by telling a story of how her husband doesn't really "get it" either or that her own kid did something even worse then yours. Women get it. They understand the pain. Sisterhood is a wonderful thing.

How Chris and I got to Phillipstown was nothing special in itself, but knowing now the direction of things to come, it was actually one of those "a-ha!" moments. Life is full of them, but we seldom see them at the time. We can always look back on a lifetime and see the connections, and yet, when in the midst of it, we are often too caught up in the day to day moments of our lives and too busy to recognize things of importance. That certainly was the case when we first considered calling this sleepy little town our home. It was not a great place in the sense of what it offered, but the houses were in our price range and when you are twenty-two and buying your first home, price is everything. Most of the mills had closed down years before and much of downtown reflected the unkempt grandeur of days past. Old mansions built by founding fathers were neighbors to the ugly urban renewal of the 70's. On any given corner the inevitable Dunkin' Donuts or McDonalds flashed neon nonsense onto brick buildings that deserved a more stately dignity. It was a working class sort of town, experiencing the housing boom of the mid 80's when many of the "people from away" came to town. Housing developments and random capes and ranches were over taking the rural roads that were once home to family owned blueberry farms or woods beloved by hunters.

Having been married for three years, Chris and I decided it was time to try and buy our first real home. Our exciting "love at first sight relationship" had begun as it does for many young naive couples, but shortly thereafter, real life took hold. Money was tight, and as we lived with each other, differences in our way of thinking began to creep in to rock the picture perfect life I had envisioned. It's true. I was a dreamer who held some unrealistic, adolescent view of Prince Charming and "living happily ever after." Chris was a worrier; I kept searching for the American dream. We had lived in a teeny, tiny one-bedroom apartment and then had moved into a small mobile home with the help of Chris' family. I gave birth to our son Adam a little over a year after the wedding. He was a beautiful little boy with brown hair and brown eyes and from the moment I met him, he was my greatest joy and one of my most profound achievements. Perhaps it was my very naiveté that protected me in the beginning. In many ways I didn't know better and so, in spite of the challenges that Chris and I faced, I just figured that this was what life was supposed to be all about.

Although originally we had hoped to live near Portsmouth, New Hampshire, we realized early on that the seacoast area was way out of our nominal price range. So we expanded our search, little by little traveling up Route 236, heading north into Maine, through South Berwick and up Route 4, until finally we came to a place where banks were willing to talk to us and opportunity knocked. It took thirty miles of road to get there, but that seemed a small price to pay in the long run. We settled on building a small split-level home on an acre of land in the outskirts of Phillipstown near the airport. There, nestled among pine trees and a running stream, was a small slice of heaven that was to become our home.

July 23, 1985

We found the perfect house! It's not actually built yet, but the realtor showed us the plans and drove us out to see the property. Phillipstown is about 30 miles north of Portsmouth and seems to have a lot to offer. It is not out in the "boonies" like I first thought. After growing up in Northwood, I don't want to be without a place to grocery shop or go to a movie. The property is on the south side of town near the airport and is very rural, but within 10 minutes of all the conveniences. Our house will be a split-level style, which was never my favorite, but it will give us the most space for the least amount of money. We'll have a kitchen, living room, bathroom and two bedrooms. Downstairs will be unfinished and we can make this room into living space someday. We'll have an acre of land and everything! I'm so excited! I'm already picking out the colors I want and am thinking about how I will decorate it! I still can't believe that we will have a brand new house. I've never lived in a brand new house before! Adam will have his own bedroom and yard to play in. I just can't believe it is all going to work out. We went to the

bank and are pre-approved for a Maine State Housing's loan of
$42,000! We are so lucky!

I had no idea, of course, what this town would come
to mean in my life. Without it, I wouldn't have met my
friends, made the decisions I made, and perhaps, would
not even have lived my life to tell this story. People
often embark on one road thinking that it will lead us
in a chosen direction, and then somehow along the way,
magically, we end up somewhere all together different.

At the same time that we bought our first house, the
other girls who would soon become my best friends were
also choosing to call Phillipstown home. In Maine, they
say you have to live in a town for at least twenty years
to be considered a Mainer and so now, after these fifty-
odd years, we are certainly all "official". Like many of
the people in this town, I was a transplant by way of New
Hampshire and some of the girls who would become my
friends were also originally from other states. I don't
think any originated in Massachusetts.... thank God,
because according to Maine standards that would be a
blemish of character that could only be overcome by a
change in attitude and decades of Maine living. Even
then you run the risk of being called a "Masshole". A few
of my new friends were original townies, but ironically,
over our lifetime, we all became townies.

The house next to ours was also a split-level, built
only a few months before ours. The young couple that
lived there had one little boy about three and Noelle
was pregnant and expecting her second child. Shortly
after we moved in, Noelle came by to introduce herself.
She was very pleasant and made me feel welcomed to
the neighborhood. Arriving with a plate of brownies in
her hand, and an invitation to attend a "Mother's Club"
that next Tuesday, Noelle unknowingly opened another

important door for me. She was also a young mom in her late twenties, newly arrived from the Presque Isle area of northern Maine known as "The County". She said that she hadn't known anyone in town either, but that she'd been going to this Mothers' Club every Tuesday morning at the Congregational Church up town. She explained that the great thing about the group was that they offered babysitting while all the moms had the chance to get to know one another and do things like make crafts or listen to guest speakers. Although I was a little shy about attending, I told Noelle I'd like to go. Being home with Adam full time was a great thing, but you could only watch so many hours of Mr. Rogers and Sesame Street before going insane. With an active toddler who got into mischief at every turn, I felt as though my whole day revolved around changing diapers, cleaning up messes and making sure that everything was perfect before Chris got home. Perhaps Chris made me feel the need for perfection, but I think I was just as much to blame. I often found myself wondering, if all of this was supposed to bring me happiness, why did I just feel overwhelmed?

Most of the women who attended Mothers' Club did so because they too were from "away" and they didn't have family or old friends in town. As the weeks passed, I looked forward to my Tuesday mornings and the opportunity to talk with the other women who were fast becoming my friends. Adam enjoyed playing with the other children too and being at Mothers' Club gave me a newfound sense of community.

Women can validate your feelings when you are sure that you are the only one losing your mind. When your toddler won't sleep or refuses to potty train, they always let you know that their kids did the same annoying things. We were all losing our minds together. Perhaps that is what made this connection so important. We cooked meals for each other when we were new mothers or in times of crisis, and babysat for each other at the drop of a hat. As moms, we spend so much time caring for our families that we sometimes lose ourselves in the process. At Mothers' Club, we nurtured each other.

January 28, 1986

As I sat on the couch this morning folding laundry and Adam played with his Legos on the floor at my feet, I watched in horror as the space shuttle Challenger lifted off from Cape Canaveral and within minutes of liftoff, burst into two streams of smoke! I still can't believe this has happened! Christa McAuliffe, a high school teacher from Concord N.H. was on the flight and she was going to be the first teacher in space! With so much news media to cover Christa's space flight, the entire world watched as the shuttle exploded right in front of our eyes! I am still shocked by this – I don't think I've ever had anything this tragic happen in my lifetime. I can't believe that the teacher from New Hampshire – from Concord, so close to home, is gone! I keep picturing the moment the shuttle split in two and thinking as I watched, "Is that normal?" Obviously, within seconds it was evident that something had gone incredibly wrong. President Reagan said on the news that this tragedy is "a national loss" and while that is certainly true, I think about the astronauts' families. . . Christa's family. . . and their loss. Life is bigger than my little stay-at-home world.

February 5, 1986

I'm pregnant! I'm not thrilled thinking about the whole pregnancy and infancy stage, but I know that this will be great. I really want to have a sibling for Adam and I don't want him to be an only child. I love Adam at the toddler stage. He is so much fun! Still not potty trained but that is o.k. We'll work on it. His little hugs mean the world to me and make all the other craziness seem worthwhile. It seemed to take a little while to get pregnant this time, but it all worked out. I didn't want there to be a lot of years between Adam and his new brother or sister, but this way it will be perfect! I'm due in September and so they will be just under three years apart. Chris is happy, too. I think sometimes he gets stressed out, but I understand that. He has a lot on his shoulders. He is going to night school now to get his degree, so he really is busy. I'm trying my best to be a good wife and make things nice for everyone. He needs it perfectly quiet when he studies, which is difficult with a toddler in the house, but I try. Marriage is never easy. I'm sure it's like this for most people. Sometimes I think of my sister Susan who is away at college. She is off having fun with her friends and learning new things and I'm here mowing a lawn or vacuuming or doing dishes. But she doesn't have a beautiful little boy and that is what keeps me going.

March 4, 1986

Good news! I met a new friend! And I think I have it bad? Lynn came to Mothers' Club two weeks ago for the first time. She came with her sisters who were visiting from California. She has a two year old little boy and she is also pregnant. But it's really hard for her because she moved to Maine from the West Coast and really misses her family. Her husband works at the shipyard and he is away for a month now working in Scotland. She's been home alone with her little boy, not knowing anyone and doing all the stuff around the house. Last month, her husband was away and she had to get up on the roof to get the snow off so that the roof wouldn't leak. And she's pregnant, for crying out loud! She just seemed so overwhelmed and I can't blame her. Last week I went up to her and introduced myself, gave her a Kleenex (because she was crying) and a hug. We've gotten together for coffee a few times now. She is so nice and we really get along well. She is due in October so we'll have our babies at almost the same time!

As the months passed, Lynn and I became inseparable. We spent hours and hours at each other's homes, making batches of cinnamon rolls from frozen bread dough, and eating them by the dozen. The boys played Legos together in the living room or created out-of-tune marching bands by banging on drums and playing plastic trumpets. We sat together tuning out the noisy chaos, sipping flavored coffee at the kitchen table. It's amazing that we weren't blimps, but perhaps youth was on our side. Our pregnancies disguised a multitude of caloric sins. Lynn was a pretty blond California girl who had once held the title of Homecoming Queen. Even pregnant, she had the body of an athlete. She was tall and muscular with runner's legs that had won her a college scholarship in track. Her hair was worn shoulder length and she had a small strawberry mark by her right eye, but it was her smile that stood out among her features. Lynn had perfect white teeth and a smile that was contagious. She was the type of person who carried herself as though she was truly a queen (and someday she would be) and had a way of making others think she could accomplish anything. Over the years, her gentle heart would occasionally lend itself to vulnerability; however, when Lynn was up, she was on top of the world. As far as friends go, Lynn was the best. She began this journey by my side and together we muddled through life's experiences – one adventure at a time. And in the fall of 1986, we were pretty in pink.

September 19, 1986

I can't believe my baby is a girl! I don't know why I thought for sure I was having a boy, but no! I had a girl! We named her Elizabeth and she is 8 pounds, 1 ounce, 21 inches long. We were lucky this time in the sense that I had a planned c-section. After the difficulty last time with Adam's birth, we didn't want to take any chances. He was three weeks late, 9 pounds, 15 ounces and I never went into labor! Even with the doctors inducing twice – nothing! I've always thought that if I'd been living in the olden days, probably both he and I would have died. So this time, it was much, much better. I went in at six this morning, Chris was with me (although he almost fainted – they had to have him sit down), and beautiful Elizabeth was born! I was a little worried at first because she was a little blue and they had to rush her into an incubator. I couldn't hold her right away like I did with Adam. But now she is fine, thank goodness! My beautiful baby girl! And to make things easy, they did a tubal ligation while I was there. I don't want more than two children. God gave me the perfect family – a boy and a girl.

It's been a long day and finally all my visitors have gone home. Chris brought Adam in to see Elizabeth. He was so excited that he jumped onto the bed and almost pulled out my I.V.'s. He didn't mean to, though. He said that he loved "his baby". Now I should get some rest. I'm a bit sore, but overall I feel o.k. I'm sure they will bring the baby in to nurse soon so I'm gonna try and get some sleep.

Having a newborn is both magical and miserable all at the same time. When you finally rock that amazing little person in your arms back to sleep, all the sleepless hours momentarily melt from your consciousness, but then just as quickly it's time to get up and start all over again. My perfect little daughter was pretty fussy and spit up all the time. I didn't know it then, but looking back I think she might have been lactose intolerant. We didn't really know about things like soymilk and such at that time though. Fussy babies were fussy babies and doctors would just tell you they had colic. Doctors would prescribe paregoric (some mystery drug that made babies sleep) and, not knowing any better, we would slip a dropper full into their little mouths hoping for peace. Nursing became excruciating because I developed something called mastitis, whatever that was. Who knew that you needed to nurse in spite of the feeling that your breast was going to fall off? It was all a whirlwind of sleepless nights, weight to lose, and schedules to juggle.

Lynn was right there beside me, having the same experiences. She too gave birth to a little daughter the following month and we were so happy to have girls together! It was hard for Lynn because her husband still worked out of state some of the time and she continued to miss her family in California. Our morning coffee hours continued with baby carriers at our feet and dual diaper changes in between sips of hazelnut coffee. Meanwhile, our boys amazed us with the wonders of being toddlers. Beds were made for jumping, toy boxes were made for dumping, and a toilet was just some strange thing in the bathroom that neither of them had any use for. The boys were supposed to sink the Cheerios we sprinkled into the toilet bowl to perfect their potty aiming skills, but neither had quite figured out how to do that yet.

We did all the shopping, washed all the clothes and had dinner on the table by 5 p.m. Busy was a four-letter word. Just when you thought your plate was full and could hold no more, another bomb was bound to drop, and so it was for Lynn. On a chilly March morning, I opened the door to see my best friend standing there with tears streaming down her face. In between the gut wrenching sobs, I heard the words that no new mother ever wants to hear. "I'm pregnant again!" Lynn cried! With a four month old baby girl in her baby carrier and a 2 ½ year old milk-mouthed toddler hanging on her leg, Lynn was going to have another little one! "How did this happen?" I asked, thanking God in that moment that it wasn't me! But of course the question wasn't really how it happened, but why did this happen? Fate sometimes plays its hand and perhaps it was just meant to be. Lynn, like others before her, had underestimated the power of a rainy night. And so, out of a passionate storm, Lynn's third little surprise would be born.

Days and weeks passed quickly, counted by Tuesdays and the promise of Mothers' Club. The group, which began with a handful of members, grew over time. With thirty or forty members we became a well-organized group with a president, vice president and treasurer who kept track of the dues we paid to cover the babysitting costs. Amidst our other obligations of nursery school, play groups, and life in general, we did our best to give back to our community. Hours were spent making and raffling a quilt to raise money for a family battling cancer. Miles were walked to raise money for the March of Dimes. We did the best that we could to help each other and the community.

As in any large group, some of the moms developed smaller intimate friendships with each other. While we all continued to take solace in the collective support group that was Mothers' Club, I began to develop a tighter circle of friends with a certain few. What began as a friendship between Lynn and me expanded to include Trudy, Becca, Audri, Liz and Noelle. Let's see. What can I tell you about these girls?

Petite in stature with perfect style and grace, Trudy was always the voice of reason. Trudy was exactly ten years older than I was, but never seemed so. No matter how old she became, she always looked fantastic for her age. Her claim to fame was her ability to impeccably apply red lipstick and lip liner without a mirror. She never went anywhere without perfect lips. Although she was a bit more reserved than some of us, she lightened up a lot over the years. Dependable, loving and sassy all rolled into one, she was someone who was always there for you, but without making a production out of it. Unassuming and family oriented – that was Trudy. She was a woman with wonderful, quiet determination and a true friend.

Becca was a bundle of laughs. She could make the most absurd situation funny. Bec didn't have an easy life, but in spite of the adversity she had faced both in her family and at home in her personal life, she always tried to see the bright side. Becca was addicted to coffee – literally. I don't know… I think she needed the caffeine to stay upbeat. And that girl was a whiz with home decorating. She could take the dingiest little apartment and make it home. Becca was a couple years younger than I and half my size, but for a petite person she had a whole lot of moxie.

Audri was originally from the mid-west and spoke with a hint of Milwaukee still in her voice. The best thing about her was that she was willing to go the extra mile for someone she considered a friend. She would give the shirt off her back, especially if what you were wearing was a fashion faux pas. That girl should have married rich - Audri had designer tastes, but a Maine budget. None the less, she dressed impeccably and wore Liz Claiborne with style. And Audri had the best hair! Back in those days, it was short and wavy and always perfect. The strange thing about Audri was that her big personality created the illusion of height. I would have sworn she was as tall as I and yet in reality she was easily five inches shorter… she just carried herself tall. She was an avid exerciser and loved Motown, Blues and B.B. King. Audri never held back telling things like they were, but she was also the first person to help you if you were in need.

Liz could be described as a behind the scenes troublemaker who would instigate and then innocently look like "Who, me?". When she was in a good space, she would be full of life, but often when her kids were little, she was just plain exhausted. Liz had three kids close in age who were always breaking a bone or being rushed to the hospital for one thing or another. Maybe that is why she went prematurely gray. Liz didn't seem to care though. She always had a no-fuss attitude about life in general and she embraced her graying hair in spite of numerous attempts at a hair dying intervention on our part. Tall and thin, she was youthful in every other way. She was one of the few people I knew who was totally comfortable in their own skin and never self criticized.

And last, but certainly not least, there was Noelle. The best way I can describe Noelle is cheerful, sincere and giddy. She had this amazing laugh that can only be described as a "tee hee". Noelle was born up north in Aroostook County and she was one of the few women I knew that still embraced all those country values. Noelle was great at maintaining a garden, canning vegetables and making her own bread. Her family would create all sorts of homemade gifts and she appreciated the simpler things in life. I loved that about her. She was a few years older than me, but about my size, and we often shared clothes over the years. The thing that people noticed most about Noelle was her eyes. She had exotic eyes that made you wonder if she were part Native American or Asian, although I don't think that she was. And true to her name, she had the most Christmas spirit. She managed to keep her cheer all year long!

With time and shared experiences, these women and their children were becoming extended parts of my family. Sisters, if you will. While I have two sisters of my own whom I have loved dearly, at that time they didn't have children yet and that made it difficult for them to totally relate to my "mom" experiences. My sister-friends understood me. They understood what I was feeling when my husband frustrated me or when the kids did something absurd. Having women friends who are at the same point as you in their lives and who can share your life experiences is priceless.

October 25, 1987

There is a hint of wood smoke in the air and as I sit here on the front stoop, I'm reminded that winter is creeping up upon us. The trees have all turned their bright reds and oranges. With piles and piles of leaves on the ground, Adam and I spent the afternoon making a pumpkin scarecrow together while Elizabeth watched from the comfort of her stroller. We jumped in the leaves and buried each other under a mountain of crisp color. Elizabeth laughed as we played peek-a-boo from beneath the leaves. As we stuffed an old pair of jeans and flannel shirt, our scarecrow took shape and we propped him up in a chair by the front door. Adam found his old plastic trick-or-treat pumpkin in the bottom of the toy box and we secured that on top for his head! Halloween is almost here! Pumpkins grace our doorstep and a scary skeleton hangs in the front window. I always loved this time of year as a kid! For most kids, Halloween is right up there with Christmas as far as important holidays go. I remember one Halloween when my childhood friend Linda and I changed costumes three times so we could hit up the same houses again and again! We trick-or-treated until dark, and by then our pillowcases were filled to the brim. This year, Adam is going to be a clown and I'm dressing up little Elizabeth as an adorable purple bunny! I think I'm as excited as they are!

Time passed and soon winter was upon us. Lying gingerly in her hospital bed, Lynn held her newest baby boy. The room was filled with flowers and balloons that said, "It's a boy!". Our friends had all been in to visit and the other women from Mothers' Club were all set to bring her meals for a week when she came home. She delivered naturally and must have had about a zillion stitches in places too private to mention. I felt really bad for my best friend. "I'm done…I refuse to have any more kids," Lynn declared. So being the good friend that I was and having had my own tubes tied, I casually suggested that this might be a good option. I told her that it really didn't hurt that much and it was not a big deal, but what neither of us stopped to consider was that my tubal had been done following a c-section. It was not a separate procedure. Who knew it would be that different? So, without giving it much more thought, Lynn decided to go ahead and have this taken care of while she was in the hospital. The next day, when I came back into the hospital optimistically thinking all would be well with my friend, I found Lynn lying in her bed ready to kill me. Now, in addition to all the stitches she had, she also had another incision near her belly button and her abdomen was filled with the worst gas that anyone could possibly imagine. Who knew that they filled your insides with gas when they did this procedure? Maybe it was a nervous laugh, like the kind that happens when you are at a funeral or in a library, but I just couldn't help it. I started to giggle. "Sucks to be you." By then Lynn was holding her stomach and trying not to laugh because it hurt too much. She was able to let out a painful laugh in spite of it all. "Kids are a pain in the ass," she said with tears in her eyes. We both burst out laughing!

Life was a continuous adventure for us back then. Every day held opportunity to find excitement in the mundane. During the winter months we spent hours every Tuesday after Mothers' Club at Burger King where we could let all the kids play on the indoor playground equipment. What a blessing it was! For less than $5 we could feed all the little rugrats and then smile to ourselves as they got all that pent up energy out by jumping up and down on the wooden suspension bridge. On other days we made blanket tent cities across our living rooms or went sledding down the big hill behind the gazebo in town. Spring brought scavenger hunts in the park, trips to Fort Foster, bike parades and birthday parties. With summer breezes at our back, the girls and I with our kids in tow would trek out to Drakes Island. On the wonderful cove side of the beach, we would sprawl out and take over the entire place. With each of us having two or more kids, we would use winter sleds to pull all the never-ending baby and toddler equipment over the sand out to our special spot. Little feet walked behind us like baby chicks in a row. Across the sand they toddled happily with pails and shovels held tightly in tiny hands. Lounging for hours in the warm summer sun, we took turns watching each other's kids in the water. During low tide, the water would become so shallow that the kids could walk out across the jetty to the other side and pretend that they were marooned on a deserted island. They loved that! At times it was a little scary getting all the kids safely back across before the tide came in, but Lynn was great at wading through the mud flats to round up all the kids. There, on our soft sand paradise, we appreciated just how special this friendship was. As a group we could make an ordinary day into a celebration.

July 11, 1988

What a fabulous day we had! Drakes Island was its usual picture perfect spot and as we settled into our favorite cove, we took over "our" beach. With the sun shining upon us, it felt like there had never been a better summer day! I love being at the ocean! The kids spread out in front of us. Armed with pails and shovels, Tonka trucks and Barbie dolls, they created a huge castle complex for Barbie and her friends to live in. As the little ones all played, we moms lounged in our beach chairs soaking up the rays and working on our tans. The water was wicked cold today, but the kids didn't care. They all swam regardless. Then our shivering blue-lipped babies sat wrapped in towels together and ate their Cheese Nips. As I watched them, I thought to myself, maybe the Maine tourism people have it right. . . maybe this was "the way life should be."

Around this time Maggie began coming to Mothers' Club. When I first met her, she seemed quiet and maybe a little shy. Perhaps that's what drew me to her. I was always big on "befriending" quiet people. She often sat at our Tuesday meetings working on counted cross-stitch projects as she listened to our guest speakers. The thing about Maggie, however, was that when I really got to know her, she was neither quiet nor shy. Or maybe our friendship changed her over time. To be honest, I'm not really sure. If you saw Maggie on the street, you would not have a clue that under the neatly pressed Van Heusen skirt and tucked in blouse there lurked the soul of a risk taker. Sometimes she seemed like such a contradiction. Maggie dressed conservatively, but loved heavy metal. She was a wonderful seamstress, but couldn't cook to save her life. She hated formal exercising, but loved hiking, walking and biking. She and I were different, but there were a few things that we had in common. We both loved Good 'n Plenty and Strawberry Twizzlers candy and neither of us drank wine. And the fact that Maggie, God love her, would become my partner in crime and the biggest instigator in the world. Over the years she and I would spend many hours devising ways to shake things up and make life interesting for our friends. But back in our Mothers' Club days, none of that had happened yet.

If I had to describe Maggie, I would say that her claim to fame was her beautiful thick long brown hair. God, she loved her hair! She'd smile a big smile and flip her hair off her shoulder as people who have long beautiful hair do. While she and I were about the same height of 5'7" or so, she was always thinner then I was. Maybe a size 8 compared to my 12, but I could forgive her that. She was flat, I had boobs. All's fair in life and friendship. She had long coltish legs, but was built straight like a boy. In spite of differences, there are some people that you are drawn to in life and that was true for Maggie and me. Our history together would hold moments of adventure as well as close calls, but neither of us knew that at the time.

Shortly after her brief attendance at Mothers' Club, it was time for Maggie to return to her work as a paralegal and ironically, that was our real beginning. She needed a babysitter for her adorable blond pigtailed little Elaine and I was excited to have that opportunity. Not only would Elaine be nice company for my two, but it would also bring in $100 a week to pay for groceries. On that first morning when Elaine came to spend the day, she clung to my leg and had little interest in playing with Elizabeth or Adam. I think Elizabeth frightened her, but I suppose I can't blame her. Elizabeth was a bit of a wild child…cute as a button, but easy to tantrum and always mischievous. That first afternoon Lynn and her three also came over to visit. Her advice was to tell Maggie that it wouldn't work out. How could I get anything accomplished with a four year old hanging on me? Time passed, however, as it always does, and slowly but surely little Elaine became a part of my extended family. What began with uncertainty between Elaine and Elizabeth would prove to be the beginning of a lifelong friendship.

With the personal struggles I found in my marriage and in myself, I had many moments in which I contemplated leaving Chris because of our differences. My friends were my support and the ones who were keeping me grounded. They were my sanity. I was happy when I was with the kids and the girls, but at home it all seemed so uncertain. It's not that Chris was a bad person. On the contrary, he was a good man who tried his best to be a good provider, but in my mind the differences between us were becoming insurmountable. I was changing. I wasn't the same person that he had married at nineteen.

Chris had finished his schooling and graduated summa cum laude with a bachelor's degree in accounting. Now it was my turn to go back to school and, taking classes at the local college at night, I was learning to be my own person and gaining self-confidence. My friends were also teaching me not to take myself so seriously. But while it seemed I was learning to take the kids in stride, Chris was getting more anxious. He worried about the kids accidentally breaking things and would spend a lot of his time at home "checking" household items to make sure that nothing was broken. He worried about spending money. He worried that the cat might scratch the woodwork. He worried about everything. He was compelled to worry. I know now that he really couldn't help it but at that time, living that way was very stressful - at least to me.

The late 80's had brought with it the opportunity for us to buy a bigger and more "perfect" home. Initially it seemed like the beautiful saltbox style house would be too expensive, but maybe, just maybe, if we got enough selling the split-level, we could afford it. If I could figure out a way to keep to our budget, then it was o.k. with Chris. He worked his forty hours a week and left all the other household stuff to me. This was the house of my dreams and I thought surely living in a house like this would make me feel fulfilled. Perhaps then I would feel happy. As I planned out the wallpaper and color scheme, I hoped that life's perfection was just a paint can away.

September 7, 1989

As I sit here at the kitchen table with a cup of coffee and a piece of cinnamon toast, I'll take a couple of minutes to share the morning. Today was a big day in our household as it was Adam's first day of kindergarten! He was so excited to go to the big school and ride the school bus! As I watched him in his little khaki pants and striped shirt standing at the end of the driveway with his new backpack, I kept wondering to myself where the past five years had gone? He was anxious for the bus to come and kept himself busy by karate kicking the bush near the driveway while he waited. Finally as the big yellow bus appeared over the hill, he ran to his spot at the end of the driveway. I checked one last time to be sure that he had his kindergarten tag pinned to his shirt. I wanted to make sure that everyone knew he belonged in the "purple room". As I gave him a big hug and kiss and waved goodbye, I watched my son embark on his first independent journey. His little face appeared in the bus window and he waved and blew me a kiss as the bus driver drove away out of sight. I know it must seem silly, but I sat at the end of the driveway for a few minutes and cried. To watch your child begin his new life without you is both exciting and sad. It is the moment when you realize that he is no longer a baby.

As we settled back inside, Elizabeth and Elaine began watching reruns of Punky Brewster and playing Barbies together on the living room floor. I found myself sitting on the couch watching them for quite some time. Elizabeth came over to me and asked what I was doing. I swept her up in my arms and hugged her tighter then I usually do. Some days, I wish they would stay little forever. With a kiss on my cheek and an "I love you, Mommy," she wiggled to get down. Even at three, she is gearing up for independence. It seems the kids are ready, but I don't know if I am.

It's 9:00 and I wonder what Adam is doing in the purple room?

With the kids growing up, keeping up with them was a challenge. Adam had started school, but Elizabeth was a busy little girl on the go and always getting herself into trouble. She was a beautiful child, with that twinkle in her big brown eyes that gave you the hint that she would be a handful. I always said that her strong will would be an asset when she grew up, but in the meantime, parenting a child who has a will of her own can be a struggle. In contrast, Adam was a born people pleaser. He was a quiet little boy who liked to keep the peace and would go out of his way to show his sensitivity. She may have been the youngest, but when Elizabeth set a plan in motion, Adam and Elaine were just along for the ride. She often did things to get a reaction from others. I remember a time when she locked the other two kids in the garage and wouldn't let them out....they were crying and she just laughed! She'd get them to play with things they weren't supposed to like my makeup or something important that belonged to Chris. On one occasion when two other little friends came to the house to play with Elizabeth, she talked them into using permanent markers to draw on each other. That would have been bad enough, but Elizabeth drew curlicues all over the little boy's butt! How do you explain that one to the child's mom? Elizabeth always made each day an adventure. She was just that type of child.

February 19, 1990

The girls are going to drive me crazy! You will not believe what they did this morning while Adam was at school! They'd been watching the "Pippi Longstocking" video over and over when they got the ingenious idea to play out "scrubbing day". I was upstairs trying to change the sheets on the beds and I came down to see the two of them with brooms in their hands sweeping little white things all over the kitchen. They were singing and having a wonderful time, but what the heck???!!! They'd emptied the insides of Elizabeth's pink bean bag chair and were sweeping all the little mini white styrofoam balls all over the downstairs! Do you know how those little styrofoam things get into stuff? They were stuck in all the heater vents and the static made them adhere to everything they touched. I was so mad! Why do they do stuff like this? They are making me crazy! They both got sent to time out and I spent the next couple of hours trying to pick up all the styrofoam. Thank God it was all cleaned up before Chris got home!

Thank God for Lynn! Her exuberance for life continued to teach me to live for the moment and not sweat all the small stuff. She loved to be spontaneous and at the drop of a hat would think nothing of piling everyone into the car and driving the whole gang to the Children's Museum in Portland or pulling out building supplies to make a tree fort with five year olds. She never worried about getting dirty and was the first to encourage messy madness. With a little help from some finger paint, refrigerator boxes magically became clubhouses. Finger paint, toe paint, it was all good. Those kids would be covered from head to toe in paint, but Lynn didn't care. Her philosophy was that the kids were washable. God, I loved that about Lynn. We all did.

With every year that passed, the "stay at home" insanity continued. We did all we could to enjoy this moment in time with our children, while simultaneously struggling to keep our own sense of self on the days when we felt we were ready to strangle our kids for pushing all our buttons. As a mom, you beat yourself up for that one day when you totally lose your cool. It's no wonder that Chris didn't understand. Who would? To him it was all a big mystery. He did his work and came home to a neatly kept house with dinner ready, but he would be silently wondering what I really "did with my day."

In between the ups and downs, what my friends and I did with our day was never conventional. We laughed and danced and sang. We spent hours one rainy Wednesday making a music video for no other reason then to be foolish and keep all the kids occupied. Lynn and I lip-synched to the song "Hold On" by Wilson Phillips (quite a popular song that year). "Hold on for one more day" went the chorus and as we toiled in front of the camera over mounds of dirty dishes, overflowing baskets of laundry and the drudgery of housework, the kids danced with each other and jumped up and down on the couches. Trudy was our videographer and we all got a big kick out of watching it afterwards. That's just how it was. Controlled chaos. Rather than spending hours on a boring Wednesday watching TV or playing Mario on Nintendo, we always tried to make the day an adventure. I suppose my friends and I were just big kids at heart and maybe holding on to the wonder of childhood is what made it all so special.

Our entrepreneurial spirit and thriftiness was alive and well during that time, too. P.B.& J sandwiches were a staple and adding hotdogs to our boxed macaroni and cheese seemed like a luxury. We were always on the lookout for a way to make an extra buck for the family. In addition to babysitting other children, we also made craft projects and sold them to anyone interested. One of the most outrageous, yet ingenious ideas that Lynn and I ever came up with over coffee was the notion that there was great money to be made as party clowns! Kids' birthday parties were big business in those days and why not give "Chuck E. Cheese" some competition? With years of experience in entertaining a house full of our own kids, why not get paid to entertain others? Granted, we really knew nothing about being clowns, but how hard could it be? Lynn sewed some brightly colored costumes, we invested in some face paint, and took out a few books on magic and balloon animals from the library. Poof! Like the magic we envisioned, we were transformed into the world-renowned (in Phillipstown anyway) Ringo and Bingo. There wasn't a birthday party worth talking about in Phillipstown that year if Ringo and Bingo weren't there. We even took on the challenge of being the kid's entertainment at the big Pratt and Whitney company picnic. The little kids never cared that the magic tricks were lame or that Ringo (Lynn) really never knew the words to the song "I love a parade" when she'd march them around in circles. Ringo and Bingo was one of the best "crazy" ideas that we ever had.

March 15, 1990

Please God, give me strength! Do you know what they did today? Adam and Elaine were at school, but Elizabeth was home with her little friends and they were all playing nicely in the basement. I checked on them and they had out the Barbies and toys and all was fine. I went to make peanut butter and jelly sandwiches for lunch and when I went down to get the kids, I find all three of them making "soup" out of the cat's litter box! They took the poopy cat litter, the cat's wet food and the cat's water and mixed it all together and then dumped it on the basement floor! They were jumping in it! Those kids are going to make me crazy! Thank God for Lynn!!! I swear she is the only reason that Elizabeth is alive! She kept me on the phone until I could calm down. I thought I would blow a gasket! If it weren't for her

I would lose my mind. You know damn well that if I told Chris what happened he'd say "Why weren't you watching those kids?" but when girlfriends tell each other that kind of thing, they calm each other down and say "Damn kids." They get it! One minute the kids all look fine and the next minute all hell is breaking out. To women, it's not a mystery.

The bottom line was that my friends and I understood each other. We knew what it felt like to have to eat p.b.& j. every day. We commiserated when a husband forgot a holiday or wouldn't follow through on elaborately planned Valentines. We'd relate to each other on a level that our husbands, try as they might, just couldn't. We knew when a friend needed a hug or a compliment and the girls were great at providing an intervention they liked to call the Calgone moment. On really bad, stressful days we would surprise each other by arriving with a basket of Calgone bubble bath, a good magazine and flavored coffee. Then we'd pile our friend's kids and our own into the car. Double buckle everyone into the seats (as that was not illegal back then, and we didn't know as much about safety) and take off for the afternoon. To be left at home all by yourself with time to read a magazine or soak in a bubble bath was a luxury that none of us took for granted. The gift of peace and quiet. . . now that is a true friend!

Chapter Three
Times Were Changing

January 8, 1997

I finally love where I am. . . who I am. . . and who I am becoming. While today was neither exciting nor spectacular, it was actually, in its own quiet way, both. The drive home from work was filled with thoughts that made me smile. Someone told me the other day that I look really happy; I guess that's because I am. Driving down the road reflecting on things, I saw a shooting star – for the first time in my life! As it shot through the sky in the direction of my home, I thought that it somehow symbolized new beginnings . . . mine.

With the children all getting older and most of them now in school, many of the girls began either to go back to school to prepare for a career of their own or to enter the work force in one way or another. Lynn went back to school to get her teaching certificate and I was on my way to earning an associates degree in business. Our friend Audri returned to work as a registered nurse and Trudy took a part-time secretarial job in a dentist's office. Noelle opened her own tax preparation office and Liz became a high school science teacher. Some of us still went to Mothers' Club when we were able, but it didn't hold the same draw on our lives as it once had. We had each other now and we simply didn't need the larger group as much anymore. Moving on to serve as P.T.A. presidents and to chairing other committees in the schools and our community, we all kept pretty busy. A new crop of moms with toddlers in tow were joining Mothers' Club and creating their own circles of friends. Kim, Charlene, Donna, Ginger and Kitt were among the new blood at Mothers' Club and had formed their own playgroups and coffee hours that mirrored ours from five years earlier. Life is that way. A never-ending cycle of stages and experiences.

Mother's Day became our favorite holiday in those years, not necessarily because our families went all out remembering us, but because we made it our own personal celebration of motherhood. My friends and I decided that the weekend of Mother's Day would be a great time to get away, without the kids and our husbands, and we began having a yearly girls' weekend away. Initially we just went to Portland, but after a year or two, we decided that North Conway in New Hampshire's White Mountains was the better choice. Surrounded by outlet malls, great restaurants, and gorgeous scenery, what better place could a group of seven women go to get away from it all? In our getaway condo, it was all about us. We had no one else to pick up after, no dinners to cook, and no mountains of laundry to wash. It was paradise! Lounging in the resort's hot tub, we drank cocktails from large red plastic cups and laughed at how rejuvenating it was to be away from our families.

Under the glimmer of a disco ball we'd all dance together until the clubs closed down. We loved to dance! For most of us, our husbands had claimed to enjoy dancing when we had first met, but it was really just a ploy. I think, like most people who grew up during our era, even the guys held fond memories of long, slow "Stairway To Heaven" moments that graced every high school dance or prom, but generally, it was not cool for guys to dance. We had lived through the decade of disco and had emerged into the new pop culture of the 80's and 90's. Dancing and masculinity did not go hand in hand. There was consensus among us that all our guys had made gallant efforts at dancing their way into our hearts. Once a ring was securely placed on our left hand, however, each of our husbands' dancing shoes were soon traded in for a trusty TV remote. No matter. One great perk of being girls is that it is socially acceptable to dance together in a group. Decked out in what we thought were the perfect outfits, we'd take bets on which one of us might get asked to dance first. Not that we would necessarily dance with random guys, but getting noticed can do a lot for a mom's ego.

It was the 90's and our hair was big and our colors neon. For the first time in over a decade, most of us felt a little like teenagers again. We'd primp at the mirror as we got ready and share each other's clothes. Audri, with her perfect hair, would help us use cutting edge hair products and would be the first to tell us when we'd achieved hair perfection. Under the glow of the fluorescent bathroom light, all seven of us would squeeze in front of the mirror to do each other's makeup and giggle over inside jokes. Those moments together made each of us feel young and alive. We may have stood before that mirror as women in their late 20's and 30's, but our reflections captured the girls we were inside.

The best thing about being in North Conway was the anonymity factor. We could do silly things in North Conway and no one we knew was there to see us make fools of ourselves. Among the other tourists, it was easier to let our hair down. I still had to work on this concept, but the girls were helping me along. After a few cocktails or bottles of wine, pretty much any embarrassing thing became possible. We all reveled in a teenage mentality that made everything hysterical. No prank was too silly and even things that probably weren't all that comical seemed hilarious to seven women out on the town.

One night around midnight while sitting in the lobby of an expensive inn, Lynn decided that she and Becca should take a survey of all the well-dressed people to see if they liked Becca's new hat. Tired travelers were now arriving back to the inn after seeing a show or returning to their rooms from the lounge. One by one Lynn and Bec would waylay these poor people under the big chandelier to persistently ask them a litany of random questions. As self-proclaimed fashion gurus, they interviewed every person that walked past with a seriousness that was only slightly compromised by Lynn's use of a cocktail napkin to tally the results. Truthfully, I was so embarrassed that I had to go outside and wait on a bench. My friends – the fashion police! After about fifteen minutes, the inn management kicked the girls out of the lobby for harassing the guests. Lynn and Becca thought that was the funniest thing they'd ever heard! As they skipped out the door arm-in-arm, their laughter could be heard all the way out into the courtyard.

My friends adored embarrassing me. Later that same weekend, we were out driving around in Liz's "Mom mobile" (the dreaded Grand Caravan minivan). We were on our way back from a dance club around midnight when

Liz decided to turn into Shaws Supermarket parking lot. Suddenly she got the idea to use the van to stalk some poor unsuspecting guy walking through the parking lot. He probably was running in to get some late night ice cream for his pregnant wife or something equally nice and mundane, when Liz drove up next to him. The next thing I knew, Lynn was flashing her boobs out the window and my friends all hollered in unison, "My name is Laura!" at the top of their lungs. No doubt, he got more than he bargained for, and my friends achieved their goal of seeing me mortified once again. Then again, I was such an easy target!

May 13, 1990

I can't begin to tell you how much fun I am having this weekend! Being away with the girls is the perfect Mother's Day present – the gift of sanity! We've spent all day shopping and I just got back to the condo. Lynn and a few of the others are still looking for bargains in the outlet stores, but I've had enough shopping for one day! The pool and hot tub are calling my name! As we walked around together today, I kept thinking to myself how fortunate I am to have girlfriends in my life! We were laughing together and giggling over silly things. This weekend is like one big pajama party, but without all the high school drama. Here in North Conway, I look in the mirror and see a reflection of someone I've forgotten of late. I'm not the tired mom or stressed-out wife, I'm simply Laura. And that's an awesome thing to see! I hope this girl I see fights her way back into the world and stays for a while. It's good to have her back!

To decide where we would all be sleeping in the condo, we would always draw numbers to see who would share which room, so that no one felt excluded. It's hateful to have people say "I'll share a room with so-and-so", leaving some other poor person to be the last one picked. So, while the strategy was a worthy one, our decorum while performing the bed draw left a lot to be desired. It never failed. My friends would make a point of going through this number draw process while we were sitting having a nice lunch at a busy restaurant like Horsefeathers. Not that we didn't stand out enough already – seven women all sitting together at one big table, laughing and being generally noisy and obnoxious. As loudly as possible, everyone would declare who was sleeping with whom and imply to all the restaurant patrons that we were sex-crazed lesbians. How ridiculous! To imply that women who are lesbians act that way! But to my friends, it was all about creating a scene to embarrass me and back then it worked. It took nothing for my face to go scarlet. If they had done that after I got older, I'd have pulled a Madonna on them and kissed one of them right on the lips for shock value! But back in the day, I was not so bold.

It's surprising none of us ever got hurt for all our foolishness. Drinking and high heels should never go together. One late night, in urgent need to get back to the condo to use the bathroom, we were all running as fast as we could along a dark pathway that led the way back to our condo from that night's chosen club. In the lead, of course, was Lynn who still saw herself as the track star she'd been in high school. In pointy-toed spike heels she ran full speed ahead. That girl didn't do anything half way. We were all running and stumbling a few paces behind her when all of a sudden, there in the moonlight, we spied a thin wire stretched across the path to keep people from driving through. At full sprint speed, Lynn hit the wire and became airborne. Up and over the wire she flew, doing a major face plant on the tar. We should have been concerned, but drunk as we were, it seemed the funniest sight we'd ever seen! We all were laughing so hard that one of us, I think it was Becca, actually peed her pants! Lynn, however, never missing a beat, popped up like a gymnast who had just dumped her Olympic landing, but waving her hands above her head as though she'd won the gold. She should have broken a bone or chipped a tooth, but she emerged without a single injury and, more importantly, she didn't have even the tiniest rip in her favorite blue jumpsuit - and lets face it, it's always all about the outfit. Arm-in-arm, we continued on, laughing and singing along the way.

The next morning, Long Island Iced Tea hangovers were masked by Morning Mimosas, dark sunglasses, and a final marathon shopping spree to find good deals on kids' clothes or work shirts for our husbands. Sappy love story matinees ended our weekends, as we drooled over leading men and cried over happy endings before heading home to our families.

At home things were still not improving between Chris and me. His worrying was taking on epic proportions. We had the driveway paved and from then on, Chris didn't want people with pickups to park in the driveway because the tar might get dented. He also didn't want us to park in the garage because the cars might drip oil on the floor. He wouldn't let Adam have a football because he thought Adam might hit the house with the ball. I tried hard to understand him, but after eight years, my resentment was building. As strong as my feelings were, I think my husband was somewhat oblivious to them. Perhaps I didn't really let him know how I was feeling. I struggled greatly with my own sense of self. Wondering what my life would be like without him was often on my mind, but with two little children, I also questioned how I could manage on my own. Guilt continued to be a noose around my neck and the word "selfish" echoed in my ear. Who was I to feel this way? He was a good man who worked hard and never treated me badly or abused me. It was wrong to have all these feelings of discontent. Would I really be happier on my own? Back and forth went the dialogue in my head.

June 15, 1990

Who is this person who looks back at me in the mirror? I hate her sometimes. I don't know her anymore. . . or perhaps I never did. I was Daddy's little girl and then Chris' wife. I'm Adam and Elizabeth's mom. But who the hell am I??? I have tried my entire life to do the right thing, to make things perfect, to live a life that would make everyone proud, so why do I feel this way? I am nobody. Everyone thinks, perfect little Laura. Bullshit. Maybe there is no perfect and I'm just supposed to be happy. But how can I be happy when I feel like I'm suffocating. I look in the mirror and wonder what is the point. I've let everyone down. I cannot fucking be everything to everybody anymore! I am not fucking perfect! I don't fucking want to be! I look at the bottle of generic Tylenol and wonder. . .

Shut the fuck up, Laura! Don't be so damned selfish.

June 18, 1990

I just can't take it anymore. I don't want to live this way. Chris is driving me crazy and he won't let the kids be kids. Every little thing they do upsets him. If they run or play loudly, he thinks they are going to break something. I want them to be little kids! All I do around here is keep up with this stupid house, wallpaper rooms, paint the outside, mow the lawn and try to make it all perfect for everyone, but no one gives a crap. I do all the cooking and cleaning and laundry and ironing. I HATE fucking ironing! I'm the nurse, the accountant, the groundskeeper, the maid, and the cook! I'm trying to do my best, but every day is the same...do stuff for everyone else, get everyone fed and the kids ready for bed, and then go to class at USM. Chris was able to study for years in perfect silence with a fan going so that the little noise the kids made wouldn't bother him. I sit at the kitchen table with 3 or more kids at my feet, trying to write a report or read my assignment. I need to get out of here! I just can't take it. But I'm scared. I'm tired. I look at myself in the mirror and wonder who the heck would even want me anymore? I'm 27 going on 100. My mid-life crisis. People have them. Mine is just starting early.

The car was packed, the kids were strapped in, and I had every intention to leave and never return. We had clothes and toys all stacked in the Nissan Sentra and I was determined that this was it. As I drove to my parents', tears fell in a steady stream down my face, silently so that the children would not hear. I could not be married to Chris anymore, but leaving made me feel like a failure. When Adam asked where we were going, I just told him that we were visiting Grandma and PopPop for a while. Elizabeth, being only four, really didn't know what was going on. Rick Charette's cassette tape of kiddie ballads was an odd musical backdrop to my feelings of throwing it all away. It seemed so ironic. Happy children's songs had serenaded the façade I'd put forth for years. The kids were great, my friends were great, but my marriage wasn't. Chris was still at work and didn't even know that we'd left, but he'd find out in a few hours when he came home.

When we got to Northwood, however, my plan unraveled. My parents weren't home and I didn't have a key to let myself in. This was long before the days of cell phones and I really had no way of knowing how long we'd be waiting. The kids and I sat in their driveway for over an hour hoping that they'd come home. Sitting there with more time to think, I continued to cry, hoping that Adam would not see. He was such a perceptive child, though, and knew I was sad. In his little boy voice he told me that "things would be o.k." All the while, Elizabeth was getting restless… she always found it difficult to sit still for too long, and she wanted out of the car. Finally, it seemed to me that maybe this was God's way of telling me to give it one more try, and so I started up the car and headed back home. My parents never knew of my intent that day, nor did Chris. The world around me remained oblivious to my pain, and I returned to the game of pretending.

With all my friends taking on new obligations in their lives, it was getting more difficult to stay in touch with everyone on a regular basis. However, all that changed when, after a long overdue visit with her family in California, Lynn gave us the gift of "Bunko". She had been introduced to the dice game on her visit and thought this would be the perfect excuse for us to get together once a month. Instead of our old coffee hours or Mothers' Club meetings, we'd play Bunko in the evening, with everyone taking a turn as hostess. Bunko is a mindless dice game in which you try to roll as many of a given number as you can during each round. If you happen to roll three of that number in a single roll of the dice, that is called a "Bunko". It takes twelve to play this game, as you divide into three tables of four, and as you go through each round, you partner with the person sitting opposite you to accumulate points together at your table. If you and your partner win at your table, you progress to the next table, and if you lose, you stay seated where you are. But the most important aspect of the game, at least the way Lynn taught us to play, was that when you roll a Bunko, you yell and scream and make a scene in celebration. And so, our monthly Bunko get-togethers began. We'd catch up on all that was happening in our lives, enjoy a few cocktails, eat mass quantities of junk food and, oh yes, play the game. With the need for twelve players, our group of seven friends invited another cluster of Mother's Club friends to join the fun, and Kitt, Kim, Charlene, Donna and Ginger became a part of our Bunko clan.

Over the years, Bunko took on a life of its own. We measured time by when we'd see each other again at Bunko. This silly foolish game became what Mothers' Club had once been - a lifeline to help us through another month. Our connection with each other was what helped us manage the crises when our kids broke an arm, had difficulty in school, or didn't get chosen to play in the little league game. And we were also there to celebrate with each other when our kids danced in their first recital, won a prize at the art show, or took part in the school spelling bee. The bottom line was that whenever we needed someone to talk with, we girls always had each other.

As time passed Bunko was enhanced and embellished a zillion times over. Theme Bunkos gained popularity and whoever hosted that month would go all out to make Bunko night into something special to celebrate. We enjoyed Cruise Bunko, Mardi Gras Bunko, Christmas-in-July Bunko and Bridesmaid Bunko (when we all wore old, horrible bridesmaid dresses). We also introduced Bunko Barbie, adopting the little McDonald's happy meal toy Barbie as our official mascot. When someone rolled a Bunko, our little Barbie would be claimed and held on to as if she were a prized trophy. For most of us who grew up with Barbie, she symbolized perfect feminism. She could work in any career that she chose and always look stylish doing it. Our games ended with awarding prizes to the winners, and the chance to leave with a new little something just for ourselves made the game extra special. There were times, of course, when someone couldn't attend a Bunko for one reason or another and, needing twelve to play, we had a list of substitutes to call on. That was where Dale and Maggie came in.

I'd been baby-sitting Maggie's daughter Elaine for a number of years by this time and she was truly one of the family. I loved that little girl. As our baby-sitting alliance continued, my friendship with Maggie also began to grow, too. She was so much fun to hang out with. Her quiet exterior was a mask for one of the wittiest senses of humor that I have ever encountered. In March of 1990, Maggie came to me to let me know that she was pregnant again and asked if I might consider caring for her new baby as well. As you can imagine, this was a big commitment on my part because Elizabeth was already four and had just started pre-school. Adam and Elaine were in school all day and I finally had time to study during the day. Taking on a new infant would certainly change things, but Maggie had been a good friend and I really didn't want to let her down. So, after days of deliberation, I told Maggie that I would baby-sit the new little one. We had a surprise baby shower for Maggie at my house that August, and as summer turned to fall, Maggie's little Mike was born with a head full of hair and bright eyes.

So, when we needed Bunko subs. I knew that Maggie would fit right in, and little by little she began to attend the game more regularly. She brought in her friend Dale who had also attended Mother's Club way back when and finally, with the addition of Dale, our group was complete.

April 20, 1991

I hosted Bunko last night and all the girls were here! It never ceases to amaze me how much fun we have when we get together! There is an incredible energy that builds when we are all in the room and it's hard not to get sucked in. When I'm with my friends, I can be the real me. I had all the staple Bunko food – Twizzlers, Good & Plenty, chocolate for the head table, and lots of white Zinfandel for the girls! I even made jello shots for us. It was pretty funny…the more everyone slurped them down, the louder and more silly we became. I'm sure that with each Bunko that was rolled, we woke the entire neighborhood with our screams! Especially Lynn, who would hoot and holler the loudest! Our families are good sports when Bunko is at our homes. Each of us only hosts one time a year, so it's not really too big of an imposition, but still…in any case, last night was a lot of fun – I didn't win, but getting together is really what it's all about.

Most people feel blessed to share their lives with one or two close friends and yet in my circle of friends, we numbered fourteen. Having fourteen women together could be a challenge, especially when each of us had such dynamic personalities. Yet in spite of the diversity that we each brought to the group, we always managed to find common ground. While I had known our original group of friends for many years and we shared a history of raising babies together, I got to know and love our new Bunko friends, too, as they became an important part of our sisterhood.

With raven black hair and a milky white complexion, Charlene reminded me a bit of Snow White. She was a pretty girl whose claim to fame was that she had once held the title of Miss Phillipstown. Although she had won the award back in high school, she would always remain our Miss Phillipstown. She was our group's artist and professional photographer – both wonderful talents that she freely shared. Charlene was also great at organizing group games and was always a bit competitive in nature. She had a creative soul, the best manicure and a big heart.

Like Charlene, the youngest of all our friends, Kim, had grown up in Phillipstown. For years we teased her giving her the name "Princess" because she was the baby of our bunch. Maybe we were all jealous. She was the type of girl who looked innocent behind those big brown eyes, but sometimes looks can be deceiving. Kim was up for any challenge and followed through with devilish ease. She was a smart woman who held a degree in accounting and worked hard in everything that she did. When I think of her I remember Kim as someone who had a wonderful smile, loved a good adventure and a chocolate martini. She was a woman who knew pop music and shared my love for AC/DC music. She could rock with the best of us!

Now Donna. What can I tell you about Donna? Growing up in New Jersey, Donna not only had that great New York/New Jersey accent, but she was also wonderfully boisterous! With a laugh that took over the room, her presence was known the moment she walked through the doorway. Donna was also our high maintenance girl who avoided manual labor whenever possible and who loved to dote on her little white Westie dog. She was a wonderful friend whose personality was as intoxicating as the bottle of Zinfandel that she was drinking and just as spirited.

With a love of cats and all things related, Kitt was obviously named appropriately. She was a friend who never lost the art of giggling and whose laughter was contagious. A champion mom, Kitt never let the special needs of her child get in the way, becoming an advocate for him and many others. The thing that I remember best about Kitt was that she always remembered everyone's birthday and was a wonderful hostess whenever we would visit her home.

Tall and thin, Ginger stood out as beautiful among our friends. With long auburn hair and a warm smile, she was the type of girl who drew attention when she entered a room. She was a woman who carried herself with unassuming dignity. Ginger was a gentle soul, content to live in the now. She loved nature and exploring, and she was deeply devoted to her children.

And last, but certainly not least, was our friend Dale. Three words that best describe Dale are musical, insightful and knowledgeable. She was a beautiful being who sang like an angel and loved the arts. While focused on her work as a paralegal, she still found time to read incessantly, volunteer for all sorts of community committees and remain active in her church. Dale was a caring friend who was there to join in the fun and serenade us along the way.

As I finally entered the last year of my associates degree program, I decided that sitting behind a desk all day was not what I wanted. I'd come so far and it seemed a sellout to just return to the same kind of office work that I'd done right out of high school. Helping people was what I really hoped to do and so I began to explore other career options. With the help of the college guidance counselors, I finally decided to pursue a career in social work, but the path in front of me was daunting. It had taken me four years to finish my two-year degree and now I would need at least two more years for a bachelor's degree and two after that for a masters program. I wondered if I would ever get there. The kids were getting bigger, though, and I had a bit more time on my hands. Even with baby-sitting little Mike, having only one child in the house seemed like a picnic compared to the days when my own babies were that age and I traveled everywhere with a minimum of three little ones in tow.

My sisters both married during that time and our family spent a lot of time together celebrating. As my beautiful sister Beth exchanged her vows, sunlight streamed through the chapel's stained glass windows, giving hope on a bright October day. As I stood by her side that afternoon in 1992, I realized that my little sister was all grown up. The following October, with a backdrop of autumn leaves and pounding surf, it was Susan's turn to say, "I do." As her husband slipped a gold band on her finger, his eyes held hers and in that moment, I knew how much he loved her. With my sisters finding love in their lives, I wished for them all the happiness that I continued to seek for myself.

My marriage settled into what my dear friend Audri referred to as "a hum". It was all one big boring hum, lacking enthusiasm. Some couples live their whole lives that way, but I wondered in my heart if I could. After my mini mid-life crisis a few years before, I knew that I owed it to Chris to try and stick it out. The truth is he deserved better than me. I did my best to change my way of thinking, but in my heart it never really got better. We lived our lives and went on vacations and cared for the kids, but for me, there was always a void. It wasn't his fault. Chris hadn't asked for this change in me. He just wanted things to be as they had been ten years ago when he'd married that naïve little girl - the girl who wanted the perfect little family to live in the perfect little house and who thought that was where happiness would be found. However, at twenty-nine, I was realizing that true happiness must first come from within.

Some of my closest friends knew of my unhappiness, but I always tried to present a positive attitude, and so I did my best around them not to let it get me down. In all marriages there are ups and downs, and over the years

I'm sure they too struggled with issues of unhappiness, quietly stuffing that somewhere inside, and anxiously awaiting the next Bunko or North Conway excursion. In each other's company we'd commiserate over shared experiences like the forgotten birthday or anniversary or male lack of understanding. But we didn't bash our husbands...that was never what we were about. When our husbands didn't communicate, we turned to our circle of friends. When we needed an honest opinion, we turned to our friends. When we needed to feel better about ourselves, we turned to our friends. We helped each other over all those early little speed bumps in our lives, never realizing that this was only the beginning.

December 30, 1994

I can't believe this is happening to me. I'm so torn and I just don't know what to do, but I know that I can no longer stay. It's not fair to Chris. I've been in that acting class at school all semester and we just finished our group project. We had to do a play and my group chose a scene from Barefoot in the Park. The teacher paired me up with this older woman Marianne and this guy named Jake. I'm not sure what is happening to me. I know Jake likes me. I can sense it. There is an energy there that I can't ignore. It started out as no big deal – just class and sometimes the three of us would go to lunch, but now it's bigger than that. I never thought of myself as this type of person. But maybe we never really know ourselves until we are faced with certain circumstances. I don't know what to think anymore. I'm so confused. In my heart, I know that I'm interested, too. The words to Sting's new song "When We Dance" echo through my mind. How can a song so perfectly capture my turmoil? It's just not right and I know it, but somehow I don't care. I don't know what will happen with him, but if I'm having these feelings, then I can not stay with Chris. I won't put him through this turmoil again. Knowing that someone else might love me gives me the strength to leave. I'm not leaving Chris for Jake. I'm leaving Chris for myself. If I end up with Jake or someone else down the road, that's fine, but for now, I need to live on my own. To be my own person. To figure out who I really am. It's time to tell him I need to leave. I'll take the children and get an apartment or something. I don't know. . . but I just know that I can't stay. Not anymore. It's time.

Telling Chris was not an easy thing. He didn't want me to go, but I told him that I couldn't stay any longer. I was just not happy. I did the old "It's not you, it's me" thing. For the next three months, as I lay on the couch night after night, watching rerun after rerun of old James Bond movies, I tried to figure out how I would make this transition. I talked to the kids and explained to them that their dad and I would be getting a divorce, that it wasn't that we didn't love them, because we loved both of them with all our hearts, but we didn't love each other any more. The kids had heard our arguments and Adam in particular knew that I'd been sad about things, but knowing that your parents are divorcing is never an easy thing for any kid to go through. The guilt I felt about the whole thing was huge, but I'd tried hard for twelve years and spent a lot of effort trying to convince myself that it would somehow all work out. Now, it seemed that there was no turning back. I told myself, as anyone going through a divorce does, that perhaps this would be best for the kids in the long run. After all, it wasn't fair for them to grow up with miserable parents, but the truth was that I was the only miserable one.

By April, I had saved a little money from baby-sitting and borrowed some money from my dad to put a security deposit down on a small two-bedroom duplex apartment in town. My parents and my sisters were always so supportive of me and for that I was forever grateful. After apartment hunting for a few months with no luck, I had finally found something affordable that would work out for the kids and me.

Chris unfortunately thought that I would have a change of heart and decide to come back to him. He promised me that he'd change and asked me to go to counseling, but my decision was made and my mind was set. He bought me gifts and flowers that I simply gave back to him, but going ahead as planned was one of the hardest things that I ever did. Hurting him saddened me greatly. None of this was his doing and, although I tried to make it as painless as possible for everyone, divorce hurts. As the kids toys and clothes were packed, I talked about our leaving as an adventure. Since we were only moving to the other side of town, they could spend as much time with their dad as they wanted. Painting a happy picture was what I did best. In the end, I tried hard to make sure the house did not look like I had stripped it of everything important. Chris deserved the house and its contents. He had never asked for any of this.

So, leaving Chris with all the furniture except for a kitchen table and chairs, an old TV, and the kids' beds and bureaus, I moved us into our new home. Lynn helped me pack up the van and Adam was a little trooper carrying box after box as we made our pilgrimage to begin our new life. Chris was at work the day I moved and came home that evening to a note on the counter. It wasn't as if I hadn't told him, but I know he never thought I'd go through with it. I still cry when I think of doing that to him. He gave me my two very beautiful children and, if nothing else, that part of our marriage was the perfection that I'd spent more than a decade searching for.

MELINDA JOSIAH GEAUMONT

April 19, 1995

I've actually done it! We are here in the new place and I feel as though a humongous weight has been lifted from my shoulders. I'm sad for Chris, but I feel like I can breathe again! The kids spent time unpacking their things tonight and I bought them new posters for their room. They are sharing for now, but neither seems to mind. There is a large walk-in closet that we are using as Elizabeth's "play room", filled with all her Barbies and toys. I'm going to buy Adam a portable basketball hoop for the driveway. He loves basketball. It's so strange because I have almost no furniture, but I don't care! This little apartment is mine. All mine. For the first time ever in my adult life, I'm on my own. The kids can play and I don't have to worry about walking on eggshells around Chris. We can throw a nerf ball in the house and not feel concerned. I should feel scared or nervous about all this, but I don't. I feel so relieved. I can finally be myself again.

My life was changing in a big way. With the impending divorce, I decided to enroll in school full time and I also took on a part time job as an office assistant at an insurance office. I finally gave up my job of baby-sitting and even though it saddened me to think that I wouldn't see Elaine and little Mike every day anymore, it was a decision I had to make. Maggie's kids had grown to be like my own and I knew that I would still see them often, of course, but it was still a big change. It was a huge change for my kids too, as they would have a baby-sitter now until I got home from school or work each day, but they both did their best not to complain. They never really complained. In addition to my office job, I also began to work cleaning a house once a week, and occasionally on a Saturday I worked as a waitress for a catering company to earn extra money. A few times, I even sold my plasma for extra cash. In Portland they paid twenty-five dollars for a donation of plasma, which was like giving a blood donation. When my dad got wind of this, he made me promise not to do it anymore as he worried about potential risks. He said that he'd give me the twenty-five a week, but I got by without it. Between the financial aid that I received from school, my new jobs, Chris' child support, and food stamps, I was able to make ends meet. It wasn't without challenges, but I knew in my heart that it would work out.

How ironic that I went from what many would consider "having it all" to a place where I lived below the poverty line, and yet my freedom and newfound self-confidence made it all worthwhile. Material things had lost all meaning for me and it was simply having my children and my peace of mind that mattered. "Perfect" wasn't found in a house. It was found in the heart. The kids missed Chris, of course, but he had been away at work so much of the time they were growing up, I don't know how different it really seemed to them. They still saw him every other weekend and sometimes one night during the week and both kids seemed to be adjusting well.

Any major life change can rock even the most solid of friendships, however, so telling my friends about my decision was not easy. Initially, most of them tried their best to be supportive. Lynn helped me move. When Trudy's mother-in-law passed away shortly after my move, she gave me so many household items. I finally had a bed for myself and a couch, pots and pans and bed linens. Maggie stood by me even though she lost her primary baby-sitter – me! And Audri was always a rock that I knew I could lean on.

As the months passed, Jake was still very much in the picture and we had been seeing each other discretely since my move to the apartment. I wasn't yet divorced officially, but in my heart it had already been over for a long time. I was not going back to my marriage and so the final divorce paper seemed a mere formality. Jake wouldn't stay over when the kids were home, but would visit on nights when they were at their father's house.

Jake was an amazing man who made me feel things that I had forgotten I could feel. He wasn't the type of guy that one might think of as model handsome or anything, but there was a quiet strength about him. He had brown hair and hazel eyes that had an air of sadness to them, as though he'd been searching for something the past thirty-four years of life. Perhaps in me Jake finally found what he was looking for. At 6'1" he possessed a physical presence that made me feel safe. He had well-defined shoulders, a broad chest and muscular arms like those of someone who had played basketball in his younger days. I always had this thing for strong arms. He'd hold me so tightly, but with the gentlest caress he would stroke my cheek in a way that silently said he loved me. Jake was always a man of few words, but that was o.k. When he chose to say something, you knew that he meant it. His Maine coast heritage resounded in his pronunciation of words as he casually dropped an occasional "R" and replaced it with the short "A" sound. Scarborough marsh, ocean tides and clam flats were as much a part of him as the French Canadian blood that ran through his veins. Perhaps what I remember most about Jake, however, was the lingering scent of his Perry Ellis cologne mixed with his own masculinity. That smell alone made my heart skip a beat and my body flush. The old "feeling butterflies" excitement had returned to my life and what a miracle it was! I know that it doesn't last forever – not in that intense way that initially overcomes you – but when years have passed and you feel the same rush, maybe it's God's way of telling you that this was meant to be. At that time, however, I certainly didn't know where Jake and I would end up. And I suppose that it really didn't matter to me. I was taking things one day at a time.

On the very weekend that I was scheduled to go to on our annual getaway to North Conway with my friends, Jake had booked a night for us to stay at the Eastern Slopes Inn. As luck or fate would have it, the Eastern Slopes Inn also happens to be in North Conway, and so I decided that instead of canceling one or the other, that I could do both. There was no reason for my friends to know anything, as they would be staying at a condo close to Attitash Mountain. I would just plan to meet up with them the next day. Jake and I spent a glorious day together. We went for a ride and looked at Mt. Washington. We ate dinner at this little Italian restaurant where I knew my friends would not go. We avoided the big shopping outlets and we hung out by our resort pool. We'd never spent time like this out in a public place before and it felt wonderful to walk hand in hand and enjoy each other's company. That evening, however, on our way back through our hotel lobby we walked past the lounge. There, through an open door to our left, who should be sitting at a table in full view of us? My friends! Truthfully, I was panic stricken. "What do I do?" I wondered to myself, but then in an instant I knew. I had to go in and as nonchalantly as I could, introduce him. "Jake, these are my friends. Everyone, this is Jake." You should have seen the looks on their faces! It was not a good thing. Audri was probably the most cordial. She made a big point of shaking his hand and saying hello, because that is just how Audri is. She was really sizing him up, but she went about it in the smoothest of ways. The others just kind of sat there. Some said hello or gave a wave, but the tension in that room was unmistakable, and Jake and I quickly left.

The next morning, Jake kissed me goodbye and left to go back to his home. The time had come. I had to face the girls. I have never been so nervous in all my life. These were the very people that had been my lifeline for over a decade and now I wondered if they'd even still be my friends. Hindsight is everything, of course, and going to North Conway that weekend with Jake was a poor decision, but in a way, maybe it forced me to confront my friends with my new "situation". Given that many of them knew about all the years I had struggled with my marriage, I guess I didn't expect them to have a problem with my moving on, but that was naive of me. My friends, in spite of all their shenanigans, are actually very scrupulous people and in fact, I wasn't divorced and therefore I was having an affair . . . an ugly term that implies all sorts of indiscretion and yet in my heart it didn't feel that way to me. The girls whom I'd known the least amount of time seemed to have less difficulty with my situation, but some of my oldest friends struggled. Lynn and Trudy, who'd been my friends the longest, had the hardest time. I often wondered if, since their own marriages had had ups and downs and they were both sticking it out, that maybe they thought I should too. I don't really know. I stayed until Sunday that weekend, but for the first time my heart wasn't into it. I felt disconnected from the very people that I had come to count on for support. I felt like they had let me down, but in retrospect, perhaps it was I who let them down. I had compromised their sense of integrity by bringing the knowledge of my relationship with Jake into their lives.

Back home, Maggie and Audri began to fill my void. They would make a point to call me and when I was around them, there was never any judgment. They seemed to accept me and my new life. By December Chris and I were finally officially divorced. The house went to

Chris and I didn't want alimony. The only thing I took was a portion of our retirement plan. Chris had never asked for any of this and it was never my intent to take everything from him. My freedom was really all I wanted. By doing all our own divorce paperwork and filing, I was able to save us thousands in lawyer fees. Right up until that last moment, I think Chris wondered if we'd really go through with it. That evening, with the paperwork final, Audri came over to my apartment when the kids were asleep. In full Audri fashion, we had a divorce ceremony that included burning a wedding picture, saying some magical words over my wedding rings, and toasting the future with champagne. We held hands and said a little sort of prayer or blessing in tribute to my new life, my new found freedom, my independence. Out with the old, in with the new.

December 10, 1995

It's over. The divorce is final and I am officially a single woman again. I took back my maiden name and it feels great to have my own individual identity once more. I don't have any regrets about my marriage to Chris. The decisions I made were based on what I knew at the time and in truth, he was always a good person. If I'd never married him, we wouldn't have had our two amazing beautiful children who continue to bring me such joy. I've learned a lot over the past thirteen years. So much about myself and who I am. I realize that things do not bring us happiness, only connection with others and love of ourselves can fulfill us. If we don't love ourselves, no one else will be able to love us either. I've had to stop going to Bible study, which is hard because I spent so many years doing that on Sundays, but I'm not willing to stop seeing Jake and that was the church group's stipulation if I decided to still attend. I wonder if that makes me a bad Christian, but in my heart I don't think so. I believe that God understands.

I look in the mirror tonight and see myself as if for the first time. My 32-year-old face finally looks happy. I've never thought of myself as beautiful. . . as a matter of fact, I've always beaten myself up in that regard. I'm a solid size 10/12 woman with less then perfect teeth and a smile that shows too much gum. And yet tonight, I feel like I'm o.k. I'm not fat and my smile is genuine. My long brown hair looks attractive and my blue eyes are sparkling. Maybe not beautiful, but I think I like the girl I see. I'm finally free.

Time, thank God, has a way of healing old wounds and that was certainly true with all my Bunko friends. A year later, in the fall of 1996, Jake and I bought a little bungalow style house in Phillipstown and moved in together with the kids. By then, Chris had sold our old house and was living in Portsmouth, engaged to a woman named Ann. He still saw the kids every other weekend and would come up one night a week to take them out to supper.

You might wonder why I stayed in Phillipstown, but by this time, there was no place I would have preferred to be. It really was my home. I had lived there for more than ten years and my roots were deep. The kids were settled into school and had friends in town. My friends, who had really been everything to me for so long, were there, and so there was never really any question of us living elsewhere. Besides, Phillipstown had undergone some nice changes since I had first moved there. The town was growing and new businesses were sprucing up Main Street. We had a Wal-Mart, a new shopping center, and our downtown area had a bit of a facelift as well. It really had grown to be a wonderful little community. Our new house offered a little yard for the kids to play in, three bedrooms (finally the kids didn't need to share a room!), a living room, kitchen, dining room and bath. It had a one-car garage and, although it was a bit dilapidated, it even had a basketball hoop for Adam.

Jake, having never had kids of his own, eased into our "family life" slowly at first. He and I had amazing chemistry together, but being together was not just about us. If he was going to be with me on a permanent basis I needed to know that he and the kids could live together. I was amazed that he passed my test with flying colors. While Adam, who by then was twelve, was always quite easy to get along with, Elizabeth was a loving ten year old little girl who still could be a handful at times. She was the sweetest child one minute, but then would fly into a rage that was sometimes inconsolable. She'd been like that since she was a toddler and while I hoped she would outgrow it, we all learned that she did not. It wasn't that she meant to be difficult, but it was as if she'd lose all control of her emotions. Jake always took Elizabeth in stride, though, and actually had the patience of a saint when dealing with her. After a while, I would often lose my temper with her because she would push every limit to its fullest, but Jake would calmly talk her through her screaming tantrums and difficult obstinate moments. Challenging children often grow up to be amazing adults, though, and this was certainly the case with Elizabeth. It was just that the family had to be patient and help her along the way.

We loved living in our new little house and it complemented our lifestyle perfectly. It was not a big or fancy house, but when you walked in, you immediately felt at home. The kids were able to walk to school and so were able to participate in after-school activities even though I was often in class until early evening. We'd all get home in time to have supper together. Jake had finished his degree and was working for a company in Portland doing accounting work. I had finally finished my Bachelors and was working on getting my Masters in social work. We had a cat and even got a dog (something Chris would never have allowed). Our big fluffy Samoyed was far too large for our little house and yard, but we loved Sash just the same. My life had come full circle it seemed. I was settled back down, but in no way was my life a "hum", and on the drive home from his family reunion that year, Jake asked me to marry him. It wasn't a romantic proposal, as a "get down on one knee" proposals might be, but I loved it – and him - just the same.

April 9, 1997

Time flies. . . only ten more days until our wedding – Wow! Last Saturday my friends and Susan took me out to Muddy River Smokehouse to celebrate with a bachelorette party. We had a great dinner and listened to the band. The band was so loud that Susan, Lynn and I started using a less than perfect form of American Sign Language to try and talk over the music and, being a bit drunk, it was a comical sight. We were laughing so hard at our pathetic signing. After way too many drinks for me, we headed home, but oh my God, I am way too old for late night partying. I got so sick all over Maggie's van. My friends kept telling me to aim for the bag! Not good! It will be a long time before I live this one down. Oh well, I'm finally feeling better. Jake was so great with the whole thing, too. The girls just rang the doorbell at 1:00 in the morning and handed me over to him. He should have run away as fast as he could while he still had the chance, but he didn't. He stayed by my side all night and saw me through it all.

Saturday (my 34th birthday) I have an appointment for a massage and manicure which will be great. Then Susan's taking me out to lunch. Beth gave me a new outfit to take on my honeymoon. I am so fortunate to have such loving sisters. My family has always been there for me and I can't wait to have everyone all together celebrating our family wedding! One week from Sat is our big day! I can't believe it! Elizabeth and I went to have our hair stylist figure out what to do with our hair. We have an appointment the morning of the wedding at 8:00. Everything is done – just have to pack for our family honeymoon in Florida! Can't wait!

April 17, 1997

38 more hours till the big moment. . . Everyone keeps asking if we're nervous, but I'm not. Just excited. I know we will all have a great time. We picked up the tuxes tonight and got Adam's hair cut. All the last minute details are falling into place. Jake and I are only working till noon tomorrow. Elizabeth has Elaine overnight and Adam is staying at his friend's house too. Most of the packing is complete – just have to check it over and load it in the car tomorrow. I can't believe that Saturday is almost here!

Throughout this time, I continued to go to Bunko and see my friends. Little by little they learned to accept Jake into our circle. They were leery at first and I didn't blame them, but in time, he gained their trust and confidence. They knew that he really did love me. When it came time for our wedding in the spring of '97 many of my Bunko friends were invited.

On that unusually blustery, snow flurry filled April day, we gathered in Cape Elizabeth to celebrate the joining of our lives. We had a small wedding and reception at the Inn By the Sea and an intimate ceremony was performed on the staircase of the Inn. Adam was Jake's best man and Elizabeth was my maid of honor. The four of us stood in front of our closest family and friends and officially became a family. Unlike most traditional weddings, ours was not the joining of just two people, but rather four. My mom and dad were there proudly looking on, as were Jake's parents. Both my sisters and their families along with Jake's brother and sister were in attendance and a number of nieces and nephews, too. Connection had always been very important to both Jake and me. To have the support from both sides of our families meant everything to us. Adam gave a toast that brought tears to everyone's eyes as he welcomed Jake into our life as his step dad. It was a lovely celebration and it touched my heart to share it with those I loved. Jake and I danced to our song "I Was Brought To My Senses" – a song by Sting that captured what our union was all about. The words seemed to be written for us alone and to this day when I hear that song, I am brought back to the day we said "I do."

As the afternoon wore on, my friends took full advantage of their opportunity to "welcome" Jake and deviously plotted to sabotage our wedding suite as a wedding prank. As Lynn was fond of saying, "Not all memories are good ones." We used this phrase often over the years to console ourselves with the knowledge that even when good ideas go bad, at least you still have a memory that you will certainly never forget. Audri's and Charlene's husbands were the biggest culprits, but the whole Bunko crew was in on it. They got a key to the suite from my sister Susan and bribed the waiters to give them Crisco, cellophane wrap and crackers. They sneaked inside and put Crisco on every door handle, telephone handle, bathroom faucet and the toilet seat. Short sheeting the bed, crumbling crackers in the sheets, cellophaning the toilet bowl and writing the word SEX in red lipstick on all the mirrors were among their more ingenious antics.

Unbeknownst to them, however, Jake and I had planned an after party following the reception to take place in our suite. All our family and friends came back to our two-floor suite to celebrate and, boy, were they surprised to see my friends' creative handiwork! Of course they didn't know who had done this and some of the family was shocked by it all. Adam and Elizabeth had to be quickly ushered out so that they wouldn't see the red lipstick sex signs that were written everywhere. Meanwhile, huddled on the couch downstairs, my friends all sat looking guilty as hell and worrying if we'd ever forgive them. Payback can be a bitch and they knew it, but we were good sports. After his initial shock (and blaming the pranks on his own friends), Jake took it all in stride and perhaps, finally, we had moved past all the awkwardness. My friends welcomed him into the fold of craziness once and for all. It felt good to have the girls' full acceptance once again.

❧

The sun was low in the sky and afternoon had turned to evening. Auma began to tire. "Perhaps we can get together again next weekend, dear," she said. "This has been so special sharing my stories with you, Emma. It means so much to know that you are interested in hearing them." The remembering had been both sad and wonderful. A lone tear rolled down Auma's cheek in silent tribute to the girl she once was. She had forgotten how powerful those early feelings were in shaping her sense of self and she felt pride for the journey she had taken.

"As we read and share my story, I am struck with the notion that our lives are much like a painting that is only completed over the course of time. Our bodies and minds begin like a blank canvas and every experience, every scar, every heartache and every joy is like a layer of paint shaping the outcome of our final masterpiece. If at twenty I were to look upon my body as it is now, I would wonder where the scars, age spots and lines had come from. And if I had spoken to my eighty-four year old self, I would wonder where the confidence or inner strength that I have now had come from. Yet looking back, I am thankful that we don't know what the future holds or what experiences lay before us. We make our way in the world, muddling through each day and building character along the way. And it would seem, since I'm still around, that there is a little more painting to be done." Auma said with a smile and a sparkle in her eye. The journal pages were the key to unlock moments past and for those afternoon hours, time slowly crept backward.

Auma's connection to all her family was something that Emma had known all her life. Since childhood, Emma could remember many, many visits with her grandparents. She had spent endless hours with her Uncle Adam and his family and while she didn't remember them well, she had seen many pictures of her with her great-grandparents (Auma's parents) whom she had called Grammie and Pop Pop. At every family event she was surrounded by the love of aunts, uncles, great aunts, great uncles, and cousins ranging all ages. Their family was a close group who gathered often, celebrated enthusiastically, and held each other up in times of difficulty. Being connected to Auma meant that every holiday was a reason to celebrate and every day shared was a day to appreciate. Emma had spent lazy summer days swimming in Auma's pool, diving to the bottom to retrieve rings while Auma counted how many seconds it took to get them all. She and her cousins would play Marco Polo or do cannonballs into the water with Grampie Jake. He was always a big jokester. The memories of family were things she knew inside and out. They had provided the defining moments that shaped her into the adult that she had become. But as Emma reflected on all that, a thought came to her. Auma's secret wasn't her family. It was her girlfriends.

Emma's mind drifted to all of the people Auma had spoken of and wondered what had happened to the women who had been Auma's friends. Some must have passed away by now, but she wasn't really sure. To be as old as Auma meant that many of the most important people in your life would be gone before you. Your parents and aunts and uncles would surely have passed on and by the time you reached eighty-four, many of your closest friends would be gone too. Emma had never really stopped to think of things in that way before. Perhaps no one does when they are young, but, as people approach the end of their lives, it seems that this would be in the forefront of their minds. How could it not be? As she reflected on her own parents, Uncle Adam, and all the people she cared about, Emma began to understand how difficult this must be for people Auma's age.

Papa Chris had died a few years ago. Although he and Auma had divorced when they were young, they had always stayed in touch over the years for the sake of their children and over time, considered each other friends. Auma and Grampie would see Papa Chris at family functions and it never seemed uncomfortable for any of them. Time had a way of healing those early wounds and Emma knew how much that meant to her mom.

When she was growing up, Papa Chris would visit her mom's house on holidays and she loved spending time with him. It's funny what you remember about your grandparents. He was a small, soft-spoken man with silver hair who loved watching scary movies and eating pistachio nuts. Growing up having multiple grandparents had been really wonderful. As a kid it meant the possibility of extra birthday gifts, but as an adult Emma knew that it meant so much more. It meant having more people to love you and that, by far, was the best gift to be given. What a blessing it was to have them in her life.

After driving Auma home, Emma sat back on the couch and flipped through the old photo albums that lay in the pile. The pictures now held new meaning as Emma better understood the feelings behind each snapshot. Page after page captured Auma and her friends in all their glory. There were pictures of the girls and all the kids on the beach and at parties. Dressed up as Ringo and Bingo, Auma and her friend Lynn smiled at the camera. Group shots captured all the girls having fun and being silly in North Conway. Each page immortalized the true spirit of their friendship. Most of us are lucky to have one good friend. Auma had had many.

The week passed and once again Emma found herself looking forward to Sunday morning. Her son Glenn was spending the day with his grandparents and Emma had planned to go over to visit Auma. When Emma arrived at the little white bungalow, Grampie Jake was outside raking. At eighty-six, he still had more stamina than most people of sixty. "Emma, my sweet!" he said as he always did when he saw her. With a big hug and kiss, he welcomed her. Grampie was still a tall man, a little heavier than he once had been, with thinning hair that had finally turned salt and pepper. His glasses were thicker now and he'd lost some hearing in his left ear, but overall, he was as healthy and strong. His parents and grandmother had all lived well into their nineties and Grampie always figured he'd do the same. "Auma's been waiting for you," he said as he picked up his rake and got back to business.

Auma's house still looked as it had for as long as Emma could remember. The faded maroon wallpaper and white wainscoting gave the living room a homey feel and while Elizabeth had been after Auma to update the look, Auma always just smiled and said she liked it fine just the way it was. This was home. A sweet cinnamon smell permeated the air and as Emma made her way into the kitchen, she could see Auma setting coffee cups on the patio table outside. Auma loved her backyard and always maintained that this little retreat was her personal heaven. The inground pool sparkled in the sunlight as Grampie still kept it in pristine condition (with the help of a pool service when he needed them) and the vines and shrubs had grown over the fence to full maturity, creating a natural backdrop for this private paradise. As Auma saw her, she waved for Emma to come outside.

"It's so nice to have you here visiting with me! Remember when you were little and we'd spend the day together? I was always so proud of my beautiful Emma. And now you're taking time out of your busy schedule to spend a day with me. It means so much," Auma said as she kissed Emma's cheek. Her aged hand, spotted, wrinkled and worn paper thin from years of caring, reached out to touch Emma's. "I know how hectic your days are bringing Glenn to all his activities and juggling work and everything. I remember days like that myself. Thanks for making time to see your old grandmother," she said with a wink. "Did you see Grampie? He was happy that you were coming over."

After catching up over a cup of coffee and Auma's famous cinnamon rolls, Emma brought out the remainder of the journals. Sitting on the patio together, enjoying the September sunshine, they took up the journey that they had begun the week before.

Chapter Four
S.O.S. Forever

May 1, 2000

"S.O.S. Forever". Have you read that brick in the path that leads to the entrance of the Phillipstown Memorial Gym? Check it out. Hundreds of people walk past it each week on their way to watch their son or daughter play sports, but perhaps they don't notice it. They may not look down to read the commemorative bricks that lie at their feet. However like many things in life, truisms are always right in front of us if only we open our eyes to see them.

Twelve years had past since I first met Noelle and started going to Mothers' Club to be introduced to the others. It was hard to imagine that so much time had slipped by. We were all very busy with our families and our lives. Most all of us were back to working full time, but we still found time to remain active in the community of Phillipstown. Dale was on the school board and Liz was active in her church's committees. My friends all took leadership roles in their children's schools, working tirelessly as members of the band's booster club and running bottle drives for new school sports equipment. As with any group, situations change and people do move on. Kitt's husband was offered the position of CEO of a large company in Michigan and with that, she and her family moved out there. We all knew that we would miss seeing Kitt every month at Bunko. But whether at home or far away, we were all so busy that it was becoming more difficult for all of us to see each other as often as we had in the past. With the growing availability of email, however, we could share the stress of our new lives with the click of a send button and hear numerous replies of encouragement instantaneously. Distance held no power over our friendship. Whether we lived across state lines or on the other side of town, we stayed connected. Our emails developed into an art form, and every day held the promise of twenty or more emails to look forward to. Monthly Bunko games at our homes and yearly pilgrimages to North Conway continued to be highlights of our girlfriend time, but we also began to do more family activities. We took group camping trips in the summer with the husbands and all the kids and got together regularly for summer barbecues or parade watching.

As the kids became junior high and high school students, our community involvement took on new paths. We transitioned from meeting at the elementary school talent shows and science fairs to spending hours of bleacher time with our dearest of friends – cheering for each others' kids at all their sporting events – and commiserating over all our new-found worries. In earlier years, we had been there for each other to share in the trials and tribulations of raising babies and toddlers. We stood by each other throughout those early years never realizing that the hardest things were yet to come. Now with our children in the throes of adolescence, the stakes were raised. We worried about teenage driving, dating, high school parties, drinking, drugs, sex and all the scary things that were out there just waiting to endanger our babies. It's such a strange phenomenon, really. When kids are little, you have all these dreams and aspirations for them. You wonder what they will become and you are overjoyed by all the little miraculous moments. When kids are teenagers, though, all the big aspirations take second place to your hopes and prayers that they will simply get through this time safely. It becomes literally as serious as life and death. As a parent, you always want to protect them and keep them close, but when they become teens, part of your job as a parent is to slowly let them go. Being the parent of a teen can be the hardest job. As a group, however, we watched out for each other. It wasn't about ratting out each other's kids; it was about trying to keep all the kids safe. With that many parental eyes out there watching, we were our own little village, raising and looking out for each child. Through it all, I was beginning to gain greater appreciation for everything my parents went through when raising my sisters and me.

My circle of girlfriends had grown over the years and now our group seemed complete. There had been a few other women over the years who had hung out with us for a time, but collective connections hadn't lasted. It is funny to think back and remember how our special group came together. It certainly wasn't initially intended to be some exclusive group. Yet over the years, through the sharing of personal experiences and "in the vault" stories that we chose to only share with each other, we seemed to emerge that way. We weren't a sorority and we didn't really have a separate identity as such, until the day Kitt suggested that we read Rebecca Well's fabulous book <u>The Divine Secrets of the YaYa Sisterhood</u>! Reading that book was, for most of us, an epiphany. We finally knew who we were. We had always been a sisterhood, just like the four wonderful women in the book, but now we knew we had to have a name to identify us. We couldn't call ourselves a club because new people couldn't join. Audri always said that we had enough friends. Our connection was bigger than a group of friends. We were our own society. And so, after much consideration and the discarding of several worthy suggestions, Lynn, Dale and I declared ourselves to be the "Society of Sisters". The name and its abbreviation, S.O.S., seemed to capture the very essence of what we were all about! We'd spent more than a decade helping each other. And so, from that moment on, we became the Society of Sisters. Everyone knew us as such. Throughout the years we have developed all sorts of special, often comical terminology – enough that it has become a kind of exclusive Society of Sisters language. In true S.O.S. spirit, our children became Peons (small members of a society) and we hail our husbands as Do-bees (for all they "do" for their queen bees). From that moment on, our sisterhood, which now had twelve years worth of history behind it, took on a life of its own. Now, we had a name to live up to.

The Society of Sisters had come to mean so much in my life that our connection needed to be immortalized. Leaving our legacy seemed like such an important thing to do. When the Phillipstown Memorial Gym was having its revitalization project, commemorative bricks were sold to line the walkway in front of this famous town landmark. There was no question that I thought we should jump at this chance to be "written in stone" for all eternity. The gym had always been the centerpiece of town, as many of our sporting events were held there, as well as things like the high school proms and graduations. All of us had spent hours and hours of bleacher time together in the Memorial Gym as our kids grew up and it made perfect sense that we would feel connected to this place. I still smile when I think of the brick that reads "S.O.S. Forever". People walk across it every day and after all these years, our Society of Sisters holds a place in this town's history. We were here. To me that is so powerful!

The winter of 1999 began like any other. Jake and I had taken a cruise to St. John in early January, settling into our regular routine on our return. I was working as a clinical social worker for the Phillipstown school district by then and was quite busy. I loved my work and having two full-time salaries made it seem like we'd won the lottery. My job centered on providing social work services for children on the Autism Spectrum and helping support their families as well. While I had only been doing it for about 6 months, I very much enjoyed my work.

In February, however, after developing a cold that just wouldn't go away, I ended up in the local emergency room because I was having trouble breathing. That evening, the medical staff told me that I had pneumonia and I was given antibiotics to clear things up. Not a big deal, I thought, but after a week or so I hadn't improved and that's when they admitted me to the hospital. For five days the doctors struggled to get all the fluid out of my lung and I began to worry that something else was going on. They assured me, however, that things were going to be o.k. The team of doctors had run blood tests and taken x-rays and it appeared to be only a bad case of pneumonia. Finally, I seemed to improve and was sent home.

Two weeks passed and at last we found out what was really going on. The pneumonia had cleared up and all the fluid was finally out of my lung. I went back to the doctor's office for a routine re-check and follow up chest x-ray, but it quickly became anything but "routine." Audri went with me that day and as we looked at the chest x-ray together, we both noticed a large shadowy spot on the film. It was one of those moments when you know in your heart that things are just not good. We looked at each other, reading each other's minds and needing no words. There was no doubt that there was a large tumor in the center of my chest! From that moment on, my life began to spin off onto an unexpected scary path. A journey that I never imagined I would take, but one that I have since come to embrace.

Following the chest x-ray, I was sent the very next day for a CT scan and then almost immediately to the hospital to have a biopsy completed. Jake and I just sat there looking at the doctor in a complete daze. How could this be? We didn't know with one hundred percent certainty, but all of this seemed to indicate that I had cancer. As we tried to listen to the doctor, his slow motion words jumbled into a series of foggy surreal scenarios that couldn't possibly pertain to me. It made no sense. That artificial "too clean" smell of the doctor's office permeated the air as my mind wandered. I sat there wondering why they needed all those little cotton balls in the jar. Jake's nerves were getting the best of him and he had all he could do to keep from throwing up. Everything was completely bizarre. It was like everyone was talking about someone else, not me. Certainly this was a mistake or something. I just couldn't really believe their pre-diagnosis because I didn't feel ill. I had had the pneumonia, but never any symptoms or pain prior to that. It just seemed too strange.

While I waited in the hospital for my biopsy to be done, my family and friends all rallied around me. It gave me strength knowing that they were all there. Liz sewed me a beautiful fleece blanket with a heart appliquéd in the corner that all the Society had signed. "This blanket will help you to feel all our love surrounding you," they said. Each of them stood around my bed, encircling me with love and sending their "good juju" my way.

April 14, 1999

At 36, I look back on all the moments of my life knowing that I have no regrets. Every experience, good or bad, has helped shape my character and enhance my being as a whole. I have lived more in 36 years than most people do over the course of an entire lifetime. Two years ago when I married Jake I found true happiness – not just in the relationship, but also in myself. I was finally true to myself and through that experience I grew. I am incredibly thankful for every moment I share with Jake because he is my soul mate and I believe that we were meant to be together. Would I go back and change other decisions? Would I make other choices? No. I'd still marry Chris at 19 because without him I wouldn't have my two beautiful children. They represent all that was good in our relationship and although their father and I ultimately went our separate ways, they hold within them the best of both of us. I've always believed that we need to focus on now. . . today . . . because within each day are experiences to learn from, friends and loved ones to cherish and memories to embrace. I'm thankful that God has given me today.

To find out you might have cancer is a strange experience. It's as though you've leaped into a parallel and surreal universe where the people and places are the same and yet it has all become different. On April 7th, I had a CT scan. The scan itself was a little scary 'cause I ended up with an adverse reaction to the contrast material that they injected me with. I ended up with anaphylactic shock, but I was o.k. a short time later after receiving some medication. Results from the scan were slow in arriving, but Jake and I were patient. On April 12th (Happy 36th Birthday), I got home from work and Jake was already home. I asked what he was doing home so early. He told me that he had bad news. . . he'd been laid off from work. Wow! I guess I was in shock 'cause I didn't really know what to say. It was one of those moments when I wanted to be supportive, but I just didn't have the words. Within a half-hour of digesting that news, however, the phone rang and I received the fateful call from my doctor. She told me that indeed they had found an unexplained mass in the base of my lung and another in my chest. I had to go see a specialist the next morning to learn more. I hung up and thought, "Oh my God, I really do have cancer." Jake's being laid off from work didn't seem to matter as much anymore. This was life and death. That night amid lots of tears and sleeplessness, I heard Jake get up to use the bathroom. As I listened to the sounds of him being sick to his stomach, it began to sink in. This was all very, very real.

When the biopsy came back, the doctors sat down with Jake and me to tell us that I had stage four cancer. We sat there hand in hand, looking at the doctor and staring at each other in disbelief. I had a very rare condition called Thymoma which few doctors in the Portland area had ever seen. My family urged me to seek a second opinion with the doctors at Dana Farber Cancer Institute in Boston. I think back on that moment and understand how completely devastating it must have been for my parents and sisters. It's scarier to love someone with cancer then it is to be the person with cancer. . . at least that was my experience.

My dad had always been my mentor. He was a strong man with a gentle soul whom I looked up to all my life, but I never wanted to upset Daddy. I'd spent my whole life doing everything I could to make my dad proud. It's not that he wasn't proud of me. I know that he was. Sometimes, however, I felt that his standard was so high that it was difficult to attain, but perhaps that was as much my own "stuff" as it was his. I knew that my seeming vulnerable would be hard for him to handle. To know that I was sick was heart-breaking for him. My mom, however, was my rock. Unbeknownst to her, she was the silent force behind my family. Unassuming, relaxed and never judgmental, my mom encouraged me to be true to myself. Mom was my cheerleader. She let me feel like the little girl I once was and mothered my inner child while encouraging the adult side of me to grow. She would hug me in an embrace that only a mother can share and would listen to me as though what I said was all that mattered in the world. Faced with the news of my cancer, both my parents put up a strong front for my benefit, but inside they were torn apart. I can imagine how I would feel if one of my children had been diagnosed with cancer, let alone a cancer of this magnitude! I thank God that neither of my own children has ever had to experience it for themselves.

My sisters were equally devastated. While I know my precious sister Beth never wanted my protecting, there is something about being the eldest child that made it second nature to want to protect the youngest in the family. Not that she needed protection, but I've always thought of myself as Beth's guardian. When it came to dealing with my cancer, I did my best to appear strong in front of her and always wanted to ease her worry. With seven years between us, I had spent the better part of Beth's growing up years already out of my parents house, and so my love for her was always more as caregiver rather then confidante. Bringing her places when she was little and having her as my shadow was how I remembered

Beth. She was my sweet pigtailed shadow. I would do anything for her.

My sister Susan, however, was the keeper of secrets and my shoulder to cry on. If I let anyone enter my occasional personal pity party, it was Susan. She and I were playmates as children and we shared a history of secret moments and little girl dreams. Over my lifetime, there were very few people that I let my guard down with and Susan was one of them. If anyone knew the real me, it was she. Every family falls into a pattern of roles that are established from birth and once those roles are set, it is very difficult to break from that mold. I loved both my sisters with all my heart and would do anything for either one of them

While at Dana Farber, I learned what lay in store for me. Stage four cancer is the most severe level cancer that a person can have because it involves invasion of a major organ. In my case, it was my lung that had been infiltrated and my survival was in question. At that time, I believe few, if any, other people had survived this type of cancer for more than ten years. In spite of that, I felt I had to hold to the fact that no one knows what our life expectancy is. Just because I had this diagnosis, it was really no more indicative of how long I'd be around than if I was just a regular person crossing the street in danger of getting hit by a bus. Life is full of uncertainty and when it is your time, I believe it is your time. So, as best I could, I left it in God's hands. The good doctors at Dana Farber told me that I would be facing chemotherapy, radiation and, ultimately, an involved surgery that would include removal of my left lung. The strange thing is that I didn't cry. Jake still wanted to throw up, but we both just sat there, overwhelmed by it all. We drove home from Boston in silence, holding hands and hearts along the way.

April 19, 1999

It is so dark outside and the house is silent while everyone sleeps soundly upstairs. Today was our anniversary. Our second anniversary. I sit here at the dining room table with the overwhelming feeling that we may not have a third. But I can't let myself go there. When daylight comes, I will pull myself together and hold onto all the positive thoughts and energy that I will need to see me through. The energy to help everyone through whatever lies ahead. . . yet now, in the dark midnight hour, I can let my hair down (how ironic knowing that I will soon be losing my hair) and cry to myself. I don't like to let this side of me show because for the most part, it's not who I am. I'm a positive person. I do my best to see the good in situations. But occasionally, on nights like this, I cry silent tears and share my secret torment with the shadows. If the walls could talk. . . thank God they cannot. This is not real! Just some terrible dream from which I will soon wake and it will all be over. How can I have cancer? Who will be here to raise the kids? How will I say goodbye? And I don't want to share Jake with anyone else. I don't want him to move on and have an anniversary with another woman. I don't want him to share his bed or his heart. Those things are mine! Please God, don't let me die! I don't want to die. But maybe I have no choice.

Back at home, we were faced with telling the kids. That was so difficult! We didn't want to scare them and yet they needed to know what was going to happen with me and with our family. To me, this was far worse than hearing the news myself. How do you tell your children that you have cancer? How do you address the fact that you may die, without dwelling on that point? It tore at my heart in a way that I have rarely experienced since. As Jake and I spoke, Adam and Elizabeth sat there with tears in their eyes, listening as best as they could to all that we said. We talked about the changes that would occur, like my losing my hair and the fact that I would feel sick for a while. Our focus was to keep things as "normal" as possible while making a few adjustments for me along the way. We explained to the kids that we'd still be able to have friends over and do things as a family. My children said little, but as they watched me, I knew that they wondered if I would die.

After telling everyone in our extended families, the next group to tackle was the Society. That night we played Bunko and everyone was there. The Sisters knew what was to come. As the evening ended, we sat in a big circle in Audri's living room and the girls all listened intently while I told them the situation. Through a cascade of tears, I explained how I'd be losing my hair and going through chemo. Losing my hair was going to suck. I worried about losing my lung and what that might be like, but I tried to be brave. What I worried most about, though, was what would happen to the kids if I didn't pull through. As I looked in each pair of eyes I felt comfort in knowing that I could count on them all. They gave me gifts, but most importantly, they gathered me into this huge group hug, and each of them vowed to be with me no matter what the future held.

April 24, 1999

My friends amaze me. Last night was Bunko and for the first time in eons everyone was there. Bunko was, as Bunko always is, a mindless game of dice rolling and cheering, but that is not and never has been the point of our gatherings. It's about connections that we value enough to carefully maintain. It's a time to catch up and stay in touch with people we've known for almost 15 years. I think about how different we all are. Over the years, our friendship and ties with each other have taken on new shapes. I've always believed that each person gives what they can to each experience and sometimes, if things are too scary or close to home, there just isn't much to give. For many, my breakup with Chris and relationship with Jake were more than they could handle. I understand that. I can even respect it. For others, I think my actions were recognized as courageous and maybe for some there was even a hint of envy at the thought of following one's heart or living the dream. I don't know. We are all so different and yet so much the same. Maybe years of friendship (like family relationships) do that to you. After a while all that remains is acceptance. We might bitch and moan about everyday life, but in the end we're there for each other. They proved that last night. They presented me with a book about friends and a book of poems and within the pages were words my friends had written along with dollar bills. Lots of dollar bills. I have a hard time being on the receiving side of help, and for the second time in a week, I felt speechless. Some were able to use words to tell me how they felt, others simply hugged me, and others sent good thoughts my way because it was just to difficult to express themselves. And that's o.k. Maybe that's what our Society of Sisters is all about. We bring to our group different abilities and attributes, each as important as the next.

The coming months held days of chemotherapy and feeling lousy a good part of the time. It was always important to me, though, to try my best to keep a positive attitude. From the start I believed that if I was going to come out on the other side of this thing that I needed to learn to "embrace" my cancer rather than "fight" it. Fighting cancer holds a lot of negative energy and I needed to hold as much positive energy as I could. I was given the gift of this cancer for a reason. I was meant to learn something from it and whether I lived or died, none of it would be without meaning.

Jake did his best to keep my spirits up. No matter how difficult things became, he was there by my side caring for me and supporting the needs of "our" kids. I never would have gotten through it all without him. At night, as we lay in each other's arms, I was blessed with rare moments when I was able to slip back into "normal" and forget that I was sick. Feeling normal had shifted from common place to something I yearned for. Often, in the moonlit hours between midnight and dawn, I found myself awake. Too much weighed on my mind to sleep soundly. Lying silently next to my husband, I found myself memorizing the contours of his face – noticing the way his hair fell on his forehead, the bit of whisker waiting for a morning shave and the small scar on his right jaw, a reminder of a childhood sport injury. As his sleeping breath brushed my cheek, I closed my eyes in silent prayer that I would never forget him... nor he me.

All my family was wonderful. My children made me cards and wrote me notes of encouragement. My sisters made an extra effort to spend time with me and bring special "I love you" gifts when they visited. They even bought me a beautiful daybed complete with beautiful matching quilt and pillow shams to cheer up the room off my kitchen where I was sleeping. Daddy prayed with all his heart and soul and my mom brought me weekly supplies of nutritious food like homemade vegetable soup, green tea and bowls and bowls fruit salad. In spite of feeling crappy most of the time, I did my best to keep busy and live life as "normally" as I ever had.

In May, the annual North Conway weekend was scheduled and I was supposed to have my first chemo treatment the day before. I really didn't know if physically I would be able to go, but my incredible oncologist in Portland (who was such a great guy and oversaw the chemo prescribed by the Boston crew) was encouraging and told me he saw no reason for me not to go. After talking it over with Jake, I figured what the heck. If I was feeling lousy, I might as well feel lousy around my friends. I'd have all my Sisters to look after me.

Maggie's van was packed, but with a spot for me to lie down during the trip, and armed with my nausea medication, I headed to North Conway with all the girls. By the time we arrived at the condo I was already exhausted, but one by one all the girls took turns waiting on me. Audri, being an RN, was able to monitor my condition with reassuring expertise. They were all so terrific. As the day wore on nausea set in and I began to have pains in my legs far greater than I could have imagined. My body was rebelling against the large cocktail of chemo meds it had been given, a powerful combination of pills and drugs administered intravenously. I had spent the better part of the day prior at the Cancer Center sitting in a room that might look at first glance like just a waiting room, complete with TVs and magazines and lounge chairs. But, upon further investigation, the i.v. poles were a good hint that you weren't in Kansas anymore. You had entered the "cancer zone". In addition to the chemo meds I took other pills that were supposed to help with all the side effects.

As the afternoon turned to evening, the girls doted on me and kept debating whether or not they should go out that night. Going out dancing was a crucial part of our North Conway experience and, while there was no way I was able to go, I insisted they should go out without me. I wanted to hear all their war stories when they returned and I assured them that I'd be fine. Besides, Maggie, Ginger, Dale and Trudy were going to stay behind with me and so finally the others decided that they would go.

Since I was staying back at the condo Lynn decided that the best thing she could do given the circumstance was to make me laugh as only she could. She proceeded to put together this absolutely ridiculous outfit and when others dared her to wear it out to a club, she jumped at the chance to "carry the torch", as we used to say, and go for it. With an oversized pair of gray sweatpants as her main attire, she pulled the waistband up and over her chest creating the most hideous jumpsuit that you have ever seen. Then, she added a gaudy belt tied around her middle. As the finishing touch, she threw on a plaid jacket that she borrowed from Dale and stuck a floppy hat on her head. She bought fake tattoos (as this was before any of us sported real ones) and she placed a tattoo on her chest just above the "jumpsuit" top. She walked over to my bed, strutting like a runway model and in spite of my pain, I couldn't help laughing. "You are not going out like that!" I said, but with a mischievous giggle, she said "Yes, I am!" She had achieved her goal - I was smiling. "Make sure you guys take tons of pictures," I said as they went out the door.

That evening while the girls danced and Lynn braved facing a million snickers and odd stares, I stayed back at the condo wrapped in the blanket that the girls had given me. Maggie, Ginger, Dale and Trudy were good friends to stay behind. Maggie had been my close friend for a long time. She was always there for me. We really had a lot in common. Both of us had been quiet and a bit reserved, but over time, we both emerged quite confident and we enjoyed instigating each other. We often joked that she was the Robin to my Batman and we loved our partnership. We were a dynamic duo and our years together had brought vibrancy to our lives. That evening, while the others were whooping it up, doing God knows what, Maggie devised a plan that on their return, she would somehow sneak up on Audri and put self-tanner hand prints on her when she wasn't looking. Self tanning lotion was in its infancy back then, a horrible orange colored cream that made you look more like an Oompa Loompa than a tan goddess – and so it was definitely a plot to set in motion.

As the night wore on, the girls and I played cards while we waited for the others. After a while, I fell into a restless sleep, but finally at around one in the morning, loud laughter came bounding through the door. All my friends were dripping wet and laughing hysterically. "We climbed the fence and went skinny dipping in the condo pool!" they yelled in unison. I wished I had been there to see that sight. Not pretty, I'm afraid, but funny as hell. Naked middle-aged women trying to get their butts up and over a fence without doing permanent damage and giggling loudly, surely drawing attention to themselves in the process. With that, Maggie crept up to Audri and slapped the self-tanner on her legs and then ran like crazy to escape as Audri tore after her. Wonderful mayhem ensued on an evening when the best medicine was truly laughter. When we finally all settled down to get some sleep, it was Lynn who laid next to me, rubbing my back as a mother might do for a sick child. I could hear her softly crying.

Time passed and with each treatment I felt a little more worse for the wear, but I kept telling myself that feeling ill meant the medicine was working. I lost my hair, which was traumatic for me initially, but I decided early on that I would not wear an uncomfortable wig, choosing instead a number of hats, which worked just as well. It's a strange thing to lose your hair because that is where all your vanity is held. When it's gone, there is no vanity left. No bad hair days. No worries about how you look, because it's a moot point. And to think I was so self-conscious as a kid. Not anymore!

June 7, 1999

Last night my hair was falling out big time. I decided to take a shower and it became overwhelming. There was hair everywhere! Thank God I had cut my hair so short. I can't imagine going through this with long hair. When I came out of the shower, I looked like something out of a horror movie – patches of hair and then extreme baldness. It was scary. Plus there was fallen hair literally all over me! You can't imagine how it just sticks to you and won't brush off. The whole scene was something out of a nightmare! I'd be lying if I said I wasn't upset. As I looked at the tufts of hair that remained, I knew what I must do. I found Jake's razor in the medicine cabinet. Little by little I plastered my head with shaving cream and ran the razor over my skull. I was crying when Elizabeth knocked on the door. With grace and poise well beyond her years, my twelve year old told me it would be o.k. and helped as I tried to shave the back of my head where I couldn't reach. She was crying now, too. We were both so scared. When you look at yourself without any hair, you realize that there is just no more hiding it. The world will see you as a sick person.

I called Susan on the phone and cried for at least an hour. No matter how well you try to prepare yourself, no one can be fully prepared for the sight of their bald head. It felt awful. My family was great, though. The kids hugged me and told me I was still beautiful and that I shouldn't worry, that it would grow back. Jake said that it's only hair. He held me in his arms and kissed me as though nothing had changed. That meant more to me than he could realize. I know he still loves me no matter what. Having him as my husband is a blessing. I don't know what I'd do without him.

With the coming of summer, I would always plan our annual S.O.S. family camping trip. For the past three years, all the Sisters and their families had spent a one weekend in July together at a local campground. Each family would pack up their cars, trucks and vans with gas grills, tents, air mattresses, blenders and more food than you could possibly eat in one weekend and head to nearby Acton for our annual getaway. This year, in spite of my baldness and the cancer, we continued with our summer tradition. Camping was such a great time to sit around by the campfire and relive the stories of our adventures together, laughing and roasting marshmallows. We'd play Bingo at the campground rec. center in the evenings. The kids always loved winning the lame prizes that were awarded.

The Peons were of all ages by that time – from Kim's youngest who was only three all the way up to Trudy's oldest who was twenty. When we all gathered we had more than thirty-five kids in attendance. Many of the older ones would pop in and out, visiting during the weekend, but everyone sixteen and under usually hung out the whole time. It was a funny thing, camping. Our children had all known each other since toddlerhood, but in school and the community they were not all really friends. They were more like cousins who shared a legacy and family, but who didn't necessarily talk to each other as they passed in the halls at school. However, while camping, that all changed. The boys walked the campground together as though they owned the place and reveled in chugging contests to see who could drink the most Mountain. Dew. The pile of horrendously smelly shoes outside their tent marked their spot on the edge of our camp village. The female Peons spent time doing each other's nails and braiding hair. They could be heard giggling as the younger ones made up adventures in the woods and the tweens strolled the campground streets searching for cute boys. We all swam in the pool and played big hilarious games of softball (adults vs. the kids) with the Peons often triumphing big time over the Sisters and the Do-bees.

That weekend, as we all sat around a roaring fire, we planned a fabulous New Year's Eve party, not only to celebrate the coming of the new millennium, but also as a celebration of my recovery. When – not if – I lived they vowed to throw the best black tie party of this century. To seal the deal, my friends and I all sneaked away from the bigger group that night and walked out into the wide open field that was on the other side of the campground. There, under a blanket of a thousand stars, we laid down in the cool wet grass in a large circle. Our heads came together in the center as we all held hands and lay looking up at the universe. One by one, we took turns telling each other what we meant to each other. Good times or bad, we were sisters, not by blood, but by experience and we were the Society of Sisters forever. Together we could get through anything.

July 25, 1999

As the sun streams in across my page and I look out at my flower garden, I can't help but think, "What a glorious day!" Coffee is brewing, my family is sleeping and it's a wonderful lazy summer morning. I am ever reminded that just because one person has cancer, it doesn't take away from other people's difficulties. I mean, people can have things going on in their lives – aches, pains, problems with their kids, etc. that may not be life-threatening and yet they are equally as important to that person. I can not trivialize others' experiences, nor can I make mountains out of mine. Life gives each of us different things to handle and never more than we can withstand. And we are to embrace them and learn. I told Audri the other day that my cancer is not just about me. I believe it is a lesson to be learned by all who touch my life – my kids, Jake, my family and my friends.

When we were at the radiation center yesterday, Jake said that he thinks I'll make it because it would be too unfair for us to have only shared 4 years together. How true – I hope to spend an eternity with this man and yet I know I am forever fortunate to have had the time we've shared. I often wonder if I'll be here in the new millenium. . . I like to think I will, but sometimes I just don't know. I made each of my friends a picture collage. So many memories we share – so many laughs and a few rough spots, but yet here we are, still coming together. If we manage to see past this and I am able to Bunko into old ladyhood, we will carry these times within us. Another story to share. . . remember when. . . If I'm not here to Bunko anymore, I am confident I'll still be remembered. Maybe that's really all that anyone wants in this life – to be remembered by their friends and loved ones. To have made an indelible impression on the minds of all those you have known and to have made a difference. What a wonderful legacy to be able to have done that!

The summer had been long, but filled with many wonderful moments. We'd gone camping with my friends, spent time on Wilson Lake at a friend's camp, and gone to Florida with my sister Beth and her family. I had visited with so many family and friends and each visit was such a blessing. It was remarkable to know that so many cared. Planning my funeral was something that I felt I had to do, because I didn't want to leave it all to my family and I've always been someone who needs to be prepared. I like to be in control and yet I was learning through this lesson that it was all really out of my hands. By mid-September I had finished all my chemo and radiation treatment and was finally scheduled for my big surgery that would take place at Brigham and Women's Hospital in Boston.

Before the operation though, I was blessed with a few last minute opportunities. My dear sister Beth arranged to take me up in a hot air balloon, which was something I had always dreamed of doing. Having that moment floating above the world with her by my side is a memory I will forever hold close to my heart. From far above the beauty of the autumn colored tree line, we sailed gently across invisible currents watching our reflection in shadows cast below. I thought to myself that this must be what it would feel like to fly and wondered if angels are blessed with this beauty for all eternity. My S.O.S. friend Kim and I spent a glorious afternoon and evening on the lawn of the Tweeter Center concert venue listening to all the bands that played that summer for the Lilith Fair. It was one of the few times that I sat hatless in public and allowed the warmth of the sun to wash over my bald head. With Kim by my side, we listened as the words to Sarah McLachlan's "I Will Remember You" serenaded us and brought to mind how special our friendship was. I kept hoping that all my best friends would remember me.

The Society also came through for me. Knowing that I loved riding horses as a kid, we all decided to go trail riding one more time, just in case. It felt so great to be on a horse again, trotting through the woods on that drizzly day. All weather was good weather when you have cancer because you're just happy to be experiencing it. At least that was how I felt at the time. In true S.O.S. style, Maggie stepped up to the plate that day "carrying the torch", dressing up in an oversized cowboy hat, rope belt and ridiculous Sheriff's badge. Making me smile was their passion.

September 17, 1999

Elizabeth's birthday is only two days from now – her 13th! Such a bittersweet time for me. I love my children with all my heart and I hope that I might live long enough to see their high school prom or graduation. I just don't know.

My surgery is less then two weeks away now. I want to think that it will all go o.k. – certainly that is what the doctors are saying. I just don't know. It's hard to describe the uncertainty. I've felt for a long time that this whole experience has been bigger than myself. It's about the impact that it has had on others. The awareness, personal or spiritual, that it has given all the people who have touched my life is what it seems to be about. As people have gone out of their way to see me, I continually feel like their pilgrimage has been God's way of giving me a message. This life is about connection. We've said our good-byes without using those words and as I talk to people, like my cousins and relatives and all my friends, the visits seem somehow to have opened their eyes and given them peace in their personal lives. I can't begin to describe how many times I have left a visit or phone conversation and realized that the person I'd spoken with had gained some personal insight because of my cancer. They'd tell me that. And so, I continually think that it's not just about me – it's so much greater.

This cancer, as scary as it remains, has been a blessing. People are praying for me – many, many people. It is comforting to know that so much positive energy is coming my way. To me, that is wonderful. Sometimes it seems that my time with cancer will be done only after it's served its purpose – whatever that may be. When that happens, either I will get well or my time here on earth will be done. It's not up to me. I leave it to Him, ultimately it's out of my hands. The same is true with regard to my children. I keep having these dreams that awaken me from sleep, leaving me with this peacefulness that tells me to let it go. I sense that I have done all that I can. I've spoken to a lawyer and addressed my wishes in a will. I've spoken to Chris and requested that he might let the children remain living with Jake so as not to disrupt things more than they already would be. Especially with Chris' living in Portsmouth and being married to Ann - that would be so difficult for the kids. But I've made them no promises. I can't. I told the kids that they may have to go live with their dad, but Jake and all my family would still be there to help them no matter what happens. I've done all I can and now it's time to let it go and be at peace with myself. I've had very strong feelings lately that letting go is a part of what this experience is supposed to teach me. To have faith. This sense of tranquillity comes over me and comforts me. I sense that in the bigger picture, I (or someone – guardian angel?) will always be able to watch out for Adam and Elizabeth. I truly believe that they will not be alone.

I am so incredibly thankful for all the wonderful memories that I share with all the people in my life. I thank God for each day that the kids, Jake and I have had as a family. They are my life. I thank God for my family and my friends. And I thank God that my experience has touched so many people – that is an incredible gift that few people are given.

The surgery lasted over eight hours. My sister Susan waited with Jake in the hospital waiting room as the hours slowly passed. All my family had wanted to be there to support Jake in his wait, but sometimes in stressful situations he does better with fewer people. He and I knew that everyone back at home was fervently praying for my well-being. By the grace of God, I did survive the surgery and I spent the next twelve days in the hospital. The great news was that my doctors felt confident that they had gotten all the cancer. The bad news was that the cancer was more invasive than first thought and they had needed to remove more of me in the process. I lost my left lung, the pleural lining of my lung, the pericardium that lined my heart, two ribs, half my diaphragm (the other half now held in place by Gore-Tex, I was told) and my left vocal chord. I came out of the surgery looking much like Frankenstein's monster. I was bald and had stitches all the way down my back and across my abdomen under my left breast. In addition I had a second incision at my throat where they had wedged my now useless left vocal chord in place so that the right would be able to hit against it and allow me to speak. Truthfully, I felt as though I'd been run over by a Mack truck, but the fact that I was still living kept me smiling. My family and Jake drove down to Boston each day. The kids visited too and carefully hugged the shell of a mom they once knew. With tubes running everywhere and a body full of stitches it was a scary time, but together we held strong. My friends all traveled to Boston too, bringing me gifts. They helped Jake by cooking meals for my family the whole time. Each day, moment by moment, I gained strength and at last, it was time for me to return home.

Back at home, I was slowly, slowly recovering. My recovery was tedious at times, but little by little I learned to adapt to having only one lung. At first my breathing was quite labored, but in time that improved. My body was healing and slowly my hair began to grow back. I was so impatient - the first two months seemed to drag into eternity. It's ironic that I had had such a good attitude going through the whole ordeal of months of cancer treatment and now found myself incredibly frustrated with my slow progress. I was certainly thankful to be alive, but I just wanted to be back to my old self. Enough already! I took up cross-stitch, I read incessantly, and I drowned my days of self-pity in the music of my life long comrade, Sting.

As I rested, the girls gave me something to look forward to. We began to plan the big "Party of the Century" that had been promised months before. Like many of the S.O.S. ideas, a brainstorm had been born out of a single conversation and then grew to momentous proportion. We decided early on that, since none of us had had the opportunity to really dress up in decades, it would be awesome to dress in gowns and have all our husbands wear tuxedos. For many of us, the only times in our lives that we had ever gotten to go all out fashion-wise was at our weddings, and perhaps for some, way back at our proms.

So, it was decided, that Y2K New Year's Eve was the perfect time to get decked out. The Do-bees would wear tuxes and we would all have our hair and nails done and dress in evening gowns. It was one of the few black tie affairs that I believe ever took place in Phillipstown, at least as far as I was aware. We planned our extravaganza to take place at Audri's as she had the perfect party house. Her large home had plenty of space to hold our crowd and her living room would make a wonderful dance floor. With the right lighting and decorations, the entire downstairs would glisten! We planned out an extensive food menu as well as bar service, ending the evening with a champagne toast for all. This was to be the Party of the Century and we wanted it to live up to its name! Having the party to look forward to was a wonderful diversion for me as I recuperated.

By December, I was feeling quite a bit better and was thrilled to feel up to celebrating Lynn's 40th birthday. Milestone birthdays were often a big deal with us and Lynn's kicked off the season. We decided to "kidnap" Lynn while she was out shopping and take her to Portland to see a comedy show and then out for drinks. That evening, when Lynn and her sisters (who had flown in from California) were trying on glitzy, bargain priced gowns for the upcoming New Year's party, we barged into her dressing room at Mardens, Maine's famous surplus and salvage store, and sang "Happy Birthday" to her at the top of our lungs! What better way to turn forty than to be wearing a glamorous discounted evening gown while your friends sing to you in front of lots of strangers. It was great!

From the store, we all piled into two vans and headed to Portland. Our evening at the comedy show was a lot of laughs, but the real fun came after when we went to a club that is known for letting people dance on the bar. It was a young hip club in the Old Port area and we didn't fit in at all, but that didn't matter. With a few drinks under their belts, a number of my friends did just what they came to do. They got their middle-aged asses up on that bar and strutted their sassy little selves across the bar as if they owned the place. After a few songs the twenty-something bartender finally asked them to get down. It was not a pretty sight really and probably scared the heck out of the poor young guys who were in the bar trying to pick up young chicks. But we all thought it was hysterical! It's not often in your life that you get to dance on a bar (or "elevated dance floor" as we preferred calling it).

By the time we got back to the parking garage it was well after one in the morning and the garage was all locked up for the night! Who knew that the garages closed after midnight? Since those early North Conway days Audri's husband would remind us before we went anywhere that he'd come bail us out of jail or come save us if we ever had an emergency. He'd heard some of the stories and assumed that such a time might come. On this night we held out hope that our "get out of jail free card" would be there if we needed it, but fortunately the garage attendant finally came after we called the emergency number. We had to wait an hour or so in the frigid sub-zero Maine cold – and me with my newly equipped one lung struggling to breathe for two – but I survived and we were finally on the road home. All was well that ended well.

Before we knew it, the holidays had arrived and New Year's Eve was only a day away. Of course, back then there was all the hoopla about Y2K and the trepidation of computers crashing and natural disasters in the new millennium, but here in Phillipstown the Society of Sisters were too focused on the big party to get all wigged out by the hype. It was Charlene's suggestion, and a great one at that, to create a time capsule to mark this moment in time. We gathered at her house to deposit our most cherished S.O.S. possessions into the time capsule box. We included treasured artifacts like our original Mother's Club banner and our inspirational copy of the <u>Divine Secrets of the YaYa Sisterhood</u> with our signatures and words of wisdom written inside the front cover. I included my "Life is Good" baseball hat which had covered my bald head for the better part of a year as a testament to my new life philosophy. Lynn's contribution was her gray sweatpants that had doubled as the infamous jumpsuit back in North Conway. Each of my friends put something meaningful inside. The idea was that the capsule would be sealed and stored in the recesses of Charlene's enormous attic until twenty-five years had passed. In the year 2025 we would gather to open the time capsule together. Truthfully, back then, I wondered whether or not I would be there to see the capsule opened. Of course I was hoping for a full recovery, but I struggled with the concern of recurrence. The doctors told me that getting past the five-year point was our first hurdle and then if I could survive ten years, I'd be in the clear. Ten years is a long time to wait, but my life was teaching me patience and the importance of celebrating every day. 2025, here we come!

On the morning of our big party, all the girls met at an upscale hair salon in town for a morning of pampering and beauty. We were all there except our Kitt who was living in Michigan. We promised her we'd take lots of pictures and call her at midnight to wish her Happy New Year! With the group all there in the salon, we took over the place. The Society is a loud group to begin with, but when you added the excitement of a day of beauty, the "loud factor" increased tenfold. All the girls had manicures done – a luxury that was new to many of us. I had always been a short nail type of girl, but on that day even I got a full set done. Everyone was having fancy "updos" much like a wedding or prom, and it was so much fun to watch everyone's faces light up as they felt beautiful. I still didn't have much hair, but it was there on my head at last and curly to boot, so I was very happy. While we all became beautified, our husbands were all good sports going to pick up their tuxes. Now, you can imagine that none of the guys were really tuxedo-type men, but every single one of them went along with our plan out of love for their wives (and knowing, I suppose, that they really didn't have much choice). When it was all said and done each of our guys looked as handsome and debonair as 007.

As the evening arrived, all the Sisters, with their picture perfect hair, nails and glittery gowns, walked into the party on the arm of their handsome husbands. I felt like Cinderella at the ball. It was our special moment to shine. I'm sure there are people in California or New York that do this sort of thing regularly, but for us here in Phillipstown, it only happens once in a millennium. Audri's house glimmered with a thousand little stars that night. With strands of tiny white lights sparkling throughout each room and candlelight flickering off her grand piano, the whole place was nothing short of magical. Charlene, a professional photographer by trade, took wonderful pictures of all the couples as well group shots of all the Sisters decked out in all their finery, capturing this amazing moment in time. Our food was delicious, the drinks kept flowing and all the girls danced until they could dance no more. Even our usual non-dancing husbands stepped up to the plate and danced a few slow songs to make us happy. While all the adults partied, the thirty or more children spent time together in Audri's TV room watching movies and playing games together. When at last the ball dropped in Times Square, we raised our glasses in toast to the solidarity of our friendship and another fabulous hundred years to come!

Chapter Five
Celebration and Sadness

August 29, 2001

I can't help but think about how wonderfully things are going and how, in spite of my experiences with cancer, I've really gotten my life back tenfold. I certainly have nothing to complain about. So many doors have opened up to me and I really feel like I've been blessed. Cancer continues to hover nearby, however. I lost my friend Peggy (who attended my Cancer Support Group) last month. I am thankful that she died quickly and did not have to suffer. I was blessed to call her my friend. My own two-year anniversary is one month from today. This time of year continues to remind me of my brush with destiny. Sometimes I feel so achy on my left side and I can't help wonder if it might be the cancer returning, but I do my best to put that thought out of my head.

As the new millennium began, life proceeded for my friends and me. With my cancer behind me, I did all that I could to enjoy a new lease on life. Cancer had been a gift that finally brought me closer to inner peace. I was thirty-seven and I finally realized that people will like you for who you are and, if they don't, then to hell with them. Being true to yourself is such a liberating feeling. With a new understanding of the fragility of life, I felt there was no time to spare and it seemed important to make the most of every moment. With our big New Year's party behind us and Charlene's fortieth coming up, it made perfect sense to use her birthday as an excuse for an impromptu road trip. Charlene and Kitt had been the best of friends when Kitt had lived in town. Now that she lived in Michigan, we decided that some of us would pile into Maggie's van and drive there one weekend for a visit. Now, I know that you are thinking driving to Michigan and back in a weekend is a bit of a stretch, but our motto was that getting there was half the fun, and so we decided we would head out on our journey the following week.

Meanwhile, however, not everything was going well in Phillipstown. The year 2000 brought with it major turmoil for some of our friends. Ginger had been unhappy in her marriage for many years and it was no surprise to us when she told us that she had decided to leave her husband. In many marriages divorce is wanted by one person and not by the other, and that was certainly the case here. Ginger's decision was complicated by the fact that her husband Dan had suffered from depression over the years. With this aspect of his life changing, he fell headlong into an emotional state that he just could not escape. Ginger did all that she could to be supportive of him. It had never been with malice that she left him, but Dan began to make threats of killing himself or hurting her. We worried terribly for her safety and the safety of her boys. It was a terrifying time for all involved and there seemed so little that any of the Sisters could do but offer moral support to our friend. Ultimately, on March 1st, Dan chose the unthinkable and committed suicide.

On the very Friday that we had planned to leave for Michigan, we attended Dan's funeral. It felt surreal to be at this funeral, knowing all that had transpired in what seemed such a short span of time. Ginger told us that we should still head to Michigan – she had her family around to support her and there was nothing any of us could do. During the quiet ceremony, we all sat huddled together in a back row watching and weeping with our dear friend with the beautiful red hair, as she cried and hugged her two little sons. We all grieved with Ginger, but the circumstances surrounding Dan's death left us with a strange dichotomy of emotions. We were so thankful that our friend and her sons had not been harmed and could now move on with their lives, but we were also saddened and angered by the way it all had ended. As we changed out of our funeral attire into comfortable traveling clothes and piled into the van, it felt wonderful to be getting "out of Dodge". We were escaping.

Have you ever driven all the way to Michigan? It is one heck of a long ride! That evening after the funeral, Audri, Becca, Lynn, Charlene, Maggie and I all piled into Maggie's van and headed off into the sunset. Even under normal circumstances that kind of marathon drive could make you punchy, but leaving right from the funeral and all, the trip was destined for weirdness. We drove all night through Maine and New Hampshire, down through Massachusetts and eventually up through New York. We had decided that we would drive straight through to Niagara Falls. None of us had ever been to the Falls before and so we thought we would make a short stop there, and then head west through Canada before going into Michigan.

Audri and I did most of the driving even though we were in Maggie's van. You see, Maggie was a directionally impaired driver. That girl couldn't tell her left from her right to save her life and God forbid if she had to back up or parallel park. God love her, though, she volunteered her van and simply let us take over as we always did when it came to traveling. Eighty miles per hour was our average speed and I drove like I was on a mission. If we had stopped every time Becca said she needed a coffee we never would have gotten out of New England. Some of us may have tried to sleep now and then, but when six women are in a van for hours on end, the conversation rarely stops.

Finally after many, many hours, we reached Niagara Falls in the early light of daybreak. The sun was just coming up over the Falls and the morning mist clouded most of our view. Maggie stated that there should have been some kind of on/off switch for the mist because people drive thousands of miles to see the falls and for what? Mist! It was cold enough that the mist turned into a thin glaze of ice covering the walkways and parking lot, and just getting over to the railing to look was treacherous. The wind whipped across the frozen ground, but bundled in scarves, hats and winter coats, we gathered at the rail. We were really here! We stood together, holding hands, looking out into the mist and said a prayer for Ginger. To think that just hours before we had all been at that sad funeral made standing now at Niagara Falls quite surreal.

Denny's restaurant served an early morning breakfast that was calling our names and after a night full of eating junk food and coffee, real food seemed just what we needed. We were all so wired from lack of sleep and too much coffee and sugar, by the time we got into the restaurant. I am sure most people assumed we were all drunk. Most people are who dine at Denny's at four in the morning. Lynn began speaking in a really bad rendition of some foreign accent and slurring her words just to add to the effect. She kept telling the waitress over and over that she wanted "Moon Over My Hammie", giggling helplessly as she read the words off the menu.

It had been a long night. By the time we finally arrived in Michigan midday on Saturday we'd been on the road nearly fifteen hours. We'd driven through Canada, which Lynn kept insisting was "sooo different" just because it was another country. She thought that she was hysterical. As we pulled into Kitt's neighborhood, we drove past many beautiful, large suburban houses with perfectly manicured lawns. This was not Phillipstown, that was for sure! Seeing Kitt was great - it really felt as though no time had transpired since we'd last seen our friend and her family welcomed our crazy crew. That night we ate at a place called the Big Buck Brewery, which may not seem funny, but the whole decor inside was deer antlers. Given that Ginger's husband had been all about hunting, we felt the weirdness of this trip following us.

"Dickeyworld" is how the Society labeled any events that seemed too strange and random to be reality. Dickeyworld? The term actually first came into our S.O.S. vocabulary while on our Michigan adventure. We had visited a huge mall that was in fact part theme park and part shopping mall. It was unlike any mall that I had ever seen! In the middle was a gigantic arcade and fun park. We were all walking through the arcade when we came across a photo machine that combined two people's pictures into one, thereby creating a picture of what their "child" might look like. Of course Lynn talked me into sitting in the booth with her, but when I did, I didn't know where I was supposed to look. As I was making some stupid face and holding my head at an odd angle, the camera snapped the picture. Out of the machine came a picture of a very strange little boy, and Lynn and I lovingly referred to this unnatural child as "Dickey". Never in the history of the world had there been a more ugly child! "Dickey" was, in a word, freaky. And so the term "Dickeyworld" was born. When something was freaky and odd, we proclaimed it to be "Dickeyworld". That whole road trip to Michigan was a visit to Dickeyworld! Visiting Kitt was really nice, of course, but all the experiences surrounding it were bizarre. And once again, arising out of a conversation around a dinner table, this time at a restaurant where Bambi heads looked out at us from all directions, the idea of our Society of Sisters handbook was born and I became its author. Our list of special terms and expressions was growing and we had no doubt that an S.O.S. handbook was needed in order to capture it all as it evolved and preserve it for posterity.

March 15, 2000

It's been a busy couple of weeks here. With Dan's funeral and then our crazy road trip to Michigan, I'm exhausted! It's good to be back home. There is always something so wonderful about coming home to sleep in your own bed! The temperature has dropped again and while we've been spared bad weather of late, they predict a big snowstorm this coming weekend. What do we expect in Maine? I'll be so thankful when winter is finally behind us! I've been spending my afternoons working on our S.O.S. photo album, which is really coming along. I added all the pictures we took in Michigan and I'm pleased that many are quite funny. I'm also working on the new S.O.S. handbook. I think the girls will be amused when they see the final result. Sometimes, I crack myself up! Here are a few definitions: "Bunko Barbie" – The Society of Sister's mascot and keeper of secrets; "Society of Sisters" – A life long circle of friends who have shared laughter, tears, joys and sorrows – a true sisterhood; "The Vault" – a place where stories and adventures are stored to be shared with Society ears only; "Dickeyworld" – A bizarre parallel universe that mirrors our normal reality and twists the everyday into the obscure; "The Society Network" – looking out for each others' children, sharing information and intervening when appropriate; "S.O.S. Motto" – Everywhere and Inseparable. We certainly are that. Inseparable. And in spite of difficulties, we have a way of pulling together and making a memory out of any situation!

Back home, life continued to march on. Having had Bunko as a monthly event for over ten years, we continued to liven things up by creating a theme party atmosphere for our get-togethers. "Barbie Bunko" and "Cruise Bunko" were added to my personal favorites. On one occasion at my house we all dressed up as our favorite Barbie doll character and, as always, Maggie was the one to take it way over the top. She may not have been very politically correct with her costume – that's all I'm going to say – but she was so funny. I had a great time accessorizing our parties with matching paper goods and specialty drinks. At times, a call to dance the limbo or the electric slide interrupted an otherwise "normal" game of Bunko because, let's face it, there is never enough dancing in one's life. Creating a personal party was one of those spontaneous, wonderful things that just occurred when the girls got together. We had so much history together that any event we attended brought aspects of a "remember when" story. We had the reputation for being the life of the party and while perhaps we sometimes created a scene, it was always in a good way.

When we went out as a group, our fashion color of choice became black. Whether we were at a funeral or a wedding, out at a club or attending an important function, we took every opportunity to wear our power color. The great thing about black is that it can be easily accessorized and it always makes you look thin. Also, given our love of impromptu photo shoots, it was imperative to always be prepared and look our collective best.

On one occasion while celebrating the birthday of a friend, we decided what we really needed was our own photo calendar. Again, with a few drinks and laughs under our belts, an idea was born that would follow us for many years. That was just how it was. We'd come up with some scheme and shortly thereafter, it would happen. That year, Charlene took group shots of all of us with appropriate props acting out different monthly theme events and the first S.O.S. calendar was born. From that time on, each year one of us would put together a calendar using photos and phrases that captured all the previous year's Society events and memories.

Being a Society of Sisters was growing into something far bigger than just being friends. We had a witty language all our own captured in our handbook and a photo legacy that spanned more than fifteen years of friendship. The photo album that I kept for us was filled with pictures and mementos chronicling our history together. We really were our own society.

Ever since I was a little kid I had loved the mystery and intrigue that was associated with being part of a "secret society" and I had a ball, running with the idea that the S.O.S. was like that. Maggie and I would purposefully hide hidden messages and pictures within our album just to see if anyone would catch on and we were masters at sending coded emails. We were middle-aged women who still found fun in being silly and I loved that about us. We joked that within our group there was a "high counsel" that really made all the group decisions and guided the group. Perhaps there was, but I'm still sworn to secrecy on that one.

The most wonderful thing about us, though, was that the girls and I were never afraid to laugh or dance or make fools of ourselves. Even during times when perhaps we could have been a bit more serious, such as when visiting someone in the hospital or attending a funeral, we just couldn't help ourselves. Without being disrespectful, we always found value in focusing on the one funny story that got us through even the toughest of situations. We were masters of laughing at ourselves.

With any group as large as ours, we knew that other life challenges would undoubtedly come our way. Statistically, some of us were bound to end up divorced, some would move away, others would get ill, some of our children would have car accidents, and we assumed at least one person would end up pregnant. There is no getting around the odds of some of these things happening, but when they do, it always seems unexpected and takes us by surprise.

Overall we had great kids. Smart kids. Many were top in their graduating class, gifted athletes and artists, and they have all gone on to college and careers and done very well for themselves. But back when they were in high school, even the brightest of the bunch did stupid things. Many of our dear, sweet teenage Peons got speeding tickets, got caught drinking beer, experimented with pot, tattooed their bodies, had to go to court for minor infractions, and took up smoking. However, when their experience involved car accidents, we all just held our breath and prayed that they would be all right.

Collectively we worried and hoped that our children would all just get through their teen years in one piece. Our first scare happened when Noelle's son Alex was in a horrible car accident in which he and his girlfriend were seriously hurt and hospitalized for quite some time. Having hit a tree and totaled their vehicle, it was a miracle that neither of them had been killed. By the grace of God, both kids recovered eventually. Initially, however, Alex had a huge gash that ran across his skull, several broken ribs and serious multiple fractures to his arm. His girlfriend was comatose at first and had suffered a crushed pelvis and internal injuries. When you get that terrifying phone call from the police or the hospital, you feel like you can't breathe. To hear that one of our Peons was in such life-threatening danger shook each of us to the core. We stood around his bed in the hospital offering strength to our friend Noelle, but crying silent tears of concern. As we looked at his broken body, we remembered the little boy we had all mothered growing up. Our kids would joke that the Society was a cult because we have a name and a handbook and traditions, but when it came down to it, each of them always knew that any of the Sisters would be there for them. We would joke back with them and say, "We are the cult that cares".

We faced our children's high school years with the understanding that one of us would always be there to listen. Lynn shared a lot of wisdom about what being a teen is all about. She told us early on that when a kid dated someone exclusively for three months, a parent should assume they are having sex. We gave her grief about that at first, but as time went on, we all realized her "three month rule" was pretty accurate.

We learned lots of truisms in those years. If your child says that he has never done something, assume he's done it three times. If she says she's done it twice, she's actually done it six. Always multiply their lies by three. And lastly, assume that they are lying. Kids can't help it. When they are in high school, they will tell you what they think you want to hear and will bend the truth so they can do what they want. When you assume they lie, it doesn't mean you think they are bad kids, it just means that as a parent you must become hyper-vigilant and check up on them more. God knows we checked up on our kids. We'd go out in the middle of the night to be sure that they were where they said they were staying. We'd call the parents of their friends before letting our kids go places and snoop through their stuff, all for the sake of protecting them.

And yet no matter how much you watch and check, kids will still make some decisions that you can not stop and, again, you just hope that they make good choices. I can remember telling Maggie one day as we shopped in Macy's Department Store that I had found out my Adam was having sex. She almost dropped the sweater she was holding, completely speechless, but it was a great moment. I always knew that I could share my most secret thoughts or decisions with the help and support of a friend. Sometimes it was about getting advice, but more often it was just about having someone listen. Throughout those years we selectively shared our kids' "coming of age" stories and it was so uplifting to know that your kid was never the only one who was going through stuff.

While most all of us lived our day to day moments in Phillipstown, two more of our group decided they must move away. Ginger finally followed her heart and escaped the shadows of the circumstances that surrounded her husband's death. Phillipstown is a small town and no one easily forgets when someone commits suicide. In a courageous leap of faith, Ginger moved to Europe with her two boys to start a new life that was free from the controversy left over here in Phillipstown. She renewed a relationship with an old friend and in time married him. There are times in people's lives when they have to pursue their chance for happiness and for Ginger, this was it. We all knew that we would miss her, but we embraced her determination to rebuild a new life for her family. And with her move, Ginger officially became known as the first International S.O.S. member.

Around this same time our friend Becca finally divorced her husband of many years and she too moved away. We were not surprised by her decision, as her marriage had been up and down for a long time, but we all knew that we would miss her laugh, her love of coffee, and her ability to tell us great stories. Becca returned to her home near Augusta where her family lived and while that was not too far away, we knew that it was distant enough to keep us apart most of the time. After a short time, she too remarried and began a new life. With two more friends living away, we were determined to try and stay in touch as we had with Kitt and hold the Society of Sisters together as best we could.

April 15, 2000

There is such heaviness in my heart tonight as I sit with the news that Trudy has cancer! How can it be that after such a short time we are faced with this disease again? Perhaps due to my own experience, this news is even more difficult. Now I am on the other side of the situation and can feel the helplessness that others felt when I was sick. I hate this. The breast cancer specialists in Portland want to do a mastectomy, followed by chemo and then radiation, but I wonder to myself if maybe Trudy too should seek a second opinion down in Boston. I am sure that going to Boston saved my life and yet Trudy seems comfortable following the advice of her doctors here. It's not that I think they are bad doctors, I just wonder if the Boston people have more cutting edge information and trials at their disposal. And ultimately, I just want the best for Trudy. It is a sad, sad night in our sisterhood.

Within a year of my cancer experience our dear Trudy was diagnosed with breast cancer. As much as my cancer had been invasive, losing a breast is far more personal than losing a lung. Her doctors in Portland decided that she needed an immediate mastectomy followed by chemotherapy. Unlike my experience, which had seemed long and drawn out, Trudy faced her surgery almost as soon as she learned that she had tumors. Once again we all pulled together to support our friend.

For as long as I had known Trudy, she was always a trooper. Petite in stature, but strong in conviction, Trudy was often our voice of reason when some of us went a bit too far with our nonsense. She was also a wonderful mother and wife who never complained about things, even when she had reason to, and was never one to show self-pity. For Trudy, there was no doubt in her mind that she would beat this thing. However, we all knew that losing her hair would be a huge obstacle. Having good hair was important to her, so we chipped in to help buy her the best wig available. Along with Audri, Trudy had always been all about her hair and so we knew that this would be one way that we could support her. That evening before she went into the hospital, we all gathered together and hugged Trudy, telling her that we loved her. You can never say that too much to the people who matter.

September 23, 2000

Over the past months so much has happened. I started a cancer support group here in town because there really wasn't anything for people locally. I haven't had a big turnout, but I did meet one woman named Peggy whom I have been able to help out with rides to her treatments. Cancer seems to strike all around us. I'm more and more aware of this. Trudy was diagnosed with breast cancer over the winter and she just completed her chemotherapy, which followed her mastectomy. She lost her hair, but wears this really great wig, which I know has helped keep her spirits up. She is such an inspiration to us all. I know that she thinks about her mortality, but never outwardly admits it. She and I have talked about the experience and the side effects, though. Bottom line? Having all the cancer side effects really sucks. I think my having been through the experience helps her a little and maybe helps the others, too. It's like they know what to expect. My friends and I went to a funeral today. Charlene's father-in-law died of pancreatic cancer. In February he was fine and now he's gone. Thank God he didn't suffer for long and yet at only sixty-four his life was cut short. Charlene's dad was also diagnosed with lung cancer in February and the doctors don't give him much time. He's such a wonderful man - so friendly and full of life! Cancer strikes again. Dale's dad, too, has been diagnosed. It seems to be enveloping everyone around me in one way or another. Maybe I was just oblivious before. And sometimes I wonder why I was spared.

It seemed that cancer was striking our group from all directions. During that same year, Charlene and Dale had lost their dads to lung cancer and Noelle had lost her mom to breast cancer shortly before. Once again we tried to make a difference as the Sisters took part in "Relay for Life" fundraisers and gave what we could to the American Cancer Society. Through it all, Trudy took part in all our gatherings, as I had the year before, and never let the cancer stop her. When it was time to go away to North Conway, now it was Trudy who attended in spite of dealing with her treatments. We hoped with all our hearts that this would not be a new North Conway tradition.

In an effort to keep things lighthearted, Kitt had emailed suggesting a plan for a photo scavenger hunt. She sent us a list of different and wacky activities that we were supposed to do, capturing each of the activities on film. Then, at the end of the weekend, we'd see how many we could accomplish. Within our group, we were always pretty competitive, so we jumped at the chance to take on this challenge. Photo ops included things like sitting in a police car, standing in a fountain, wearing leather, being on stage with a band, and many other nonsensical poses. It was no surprise that we did everything on the list and we have the pictures to prove it. Amazingly, Trudy kept up with everyone the whole time and it just confirmed our understanding that laughter and "good juju" from friends can brighten even the darkest of times. In the end, Trudy lost her breast, but not her zest for life and we all continued to thank God for her.

Given my own experience with cancer and being reminded of it again through Trudy's experience, I focused my attention on creating new memories and connecting with others. With this personal commitment, if someone said that they wanted to do something, it was my new role to make it happen. I loved being a rainmaker! I can't fully describe the joy it brings me to know that I've opened up opportunities for other people. When I have the chance to share a lifelong dream with someone or can watch people I love experience something that is new and exciting to them, I feel like a small child on a wondrous Christmas morning. Moments become real-life presents, waiting to be revealed. My heart swells and a feeling of happiness abounds. Every moment is a gift yet to be opened.

At sixty-five, my mom wanted to go white water rafting and so we challenged the waters of the Androscoggin together. Later, she wanted to parasail and feel like she was flying, and so we parasailed. Jake and I took the kids to Washington D.C. and Hollywood, and on a cruise to the Caribbean. We traveled to Radio City Music Hall in New York City with my parents after they reminisced about going there in their youth. Whatever people wanted to do, I jumped at the chance. It was amazing to be given this gift of life and it felt wonderful sharing it with all those who mattered most to me. Connection was the key. I realized that money is only as good as the memories that you have to show for it and I had a wonderful time planning trips for my family and friends.

The first of our "away" S.O.S. trips was to New York City because many of my friends had never been there. In early December of 2000 we took the Amtrak train from Boston to Grand Central Station in New York City, where we spent three amazing days seeing all the sights of the Big Apple. It was so exciting to be in a place that we'd all seen on T.V. hundreds of times and to experience each landmark together. We walked to Rockefeller Center and watched the Christmas tree being put up, we watched the skaters on the ice skating rink and walked up to Central Park. Lynn asked the guy working on the big Christmas tree if we could have one of the colored light bulbs as a souvenir. Of course, he was happy to oblige, and so we walked away with a little piece of the tree lighting. We went to see the Rockettes' Christmas Spectacular at Radio City and experienced "Phantom of the Opera" one night on Broadway. We woke very early one bitter cold morning to join the crowds in the plaza outside the Today Show. With a beautiful "S.O.S in New York" sign made by Charlene, we braved the crowds and the cold in hopes that we might catch a glimpse of Katie Couric or Matt Lauer. As one might guess, it was Lynn who ended up on camera because with a big smile, she basically squeezed her way through the crowd and almost knocked over some poor old woman in a wheel chair. Lynn was on camera, jumping up and down in her cobalt blue coat, waving a toy for their "Toys for Tots" collection, practically hitting the woman in the wheelchair with every hop. It was an experience, that was for sure, and we came away knowing we had done what we set out to do - get a Sister to appear live on the Today Show.

We walked all over the city that weekend from uptown to downtown and, because I was the acting tour guide, we walked at an insane pace. It still amazes me to think of the stamina I had in spite of having only one lung, but I was always that way. Type A. Determined. And always on a mission. I think I drove everyone crazy, but we sure did see a lot that weekend. We visited the Empire State Building, cruised through Time Square, shopped in fabulous Macy's, marveling at their famous Christmas display, visited the amazing FAO Shwartz toy store and the Plaza Hotel before heading downtown toward Battery Park to see the Statue of Liberty and the Twin Towers.

When I think of that now, I realize how profound that moment was. We, the Society, had the opportunity as a group to go up in the Twin Towers in December 2000. That in itself would have been powerful, but what still remains in my mind today was the holiday message that decorated the World Trade Center courtyard that year. In front of the buildings there was a huge display erected for the holiday season that said "Peace On Earth" in gigantic ten foot tall stone letters. I know we weren't supposed to, but I had the girls all stand between the letters as I snapped a couple of pictures. There we were with the towers shining brightly in the winter sun directly behind us and the words Peace on Earth around us. Little did we know that less than a year later, it would all be gone.

How ironic that the message was one of peace and how powerful that we got the chance to experience it all.

June 18, 2001

Some amazing things have happened in my life recently! You will not believe who I got to meet! On May 25th, I had the opportunity to meet my favorite singer of all time - Sting! I was chosen as Sting's Biggest Fan by the Portland radio station Coast 93.1. I had written them a letter explaining why I was Sting's biggest fan and I later learned that all the Sisters had emailed the station as well to say why I should be chosen. I still don't know whether it was really my letter or my friends' insistence that gave me the win, but either way I was so grateful for their contribution. So, having won, I had the chance to meet the radio D.J. Tim Wright and talk with Sting backstage for almost 15 minutes. As Sting and I sat knee to knee on a comfortable sofa, we enjoyed a casual conversation as if we were old friends getting together for a long overdue visit. I kept pinching myself to be sure that the whole experience was real. He was such a nice person and I felt incredibly comfortable speaking with him. He was not pretentious as you might expect from such a celebrity, but very down to earth and approachable. We talked about my having had cancer and how his parents had died of cancer. He suggested that I become vegetarian and we talked about the importance of connection. It's funny, because I've always felt some cosmic connection with this man, although I cannot say specifically why. His music has followed me throughout my adult life and has been a presence during many important turning points for me. During our conversation, I had the chance to share with him the importance of his music in my life. He looked back at me and sincerely asked, "So, what are we going to do next?" Perhaps we are all connected in ways that we don't fully understand. When it was time to leave, he shook Jake's hand and said, "You are a very lucky man." I thought to myself, "Oh my God! Sting thinks my husband is a lucky man!" There was no greater compliment that he could have given me! It was a once in a lifetime experience and one that I will cherish forever.

The girls and I all just got back from North Conway and guess what? We all got tattoos! Well, not really all of us, but some. Trudy, Becca, Noelle, Donna and I. It was so funny. Donna had one done on her lower back and she literally fainted when the guy was doing it. She was out like a light and her gum popped out of her mouth and across the room. I caught her head in my hand – now that was funny! Being tattooed women we figure we are now "bad ass" Sisters. I love that. Mine is a cool sun and moon – it represents Jake and me and is taken from the words in our wedding song.

Jake and I have also been busy here at the house preparing for our new in-ground pool. We hemmed and hawed about spending the money, but we are both so excited about it and I am so pleased that we went ahead with things. I really think it will bring us so many opportunities to use the yard and enjoy having people over. Being with the people that we love most is what it is all about.

Life has a way of going from times of happiness to times of sadness in what seems like a blink of an eye. As we began our school year in 2001, no one had any notion of what lay right around the corner. I think back to this time and am reminded of how much changed in our lives because of this one event, not only for the world at large, but here, in my very home. And while I didn't know it at the time, we would again embark on a new journey, trying to find peace and balance along the way.

October 2, 2001

And the months continue to fly by. . . so much has happened that it's hard to know where to begin. . . September 11, 2001 brought with it terror and loss greater than my lifetime has ever known. The World Trade Center was crashed into by terrorists who hijacked commercial jet planes! I was in the front office at school when I first heard the news. I can't believe that it has happened. Tower One was hit by a plane, then Tower Two was hit by a second plane, and shortly thereafter the towers began to collapse. Those huge, huge towers crumbling to the ground while the whole world watched in horror! Meanwhile, a third hijacked plane crashed into the Pentagon and finally a fourth hijacked plane (intended for a Washington target) crashed in Pennsylvania after passengers on that plane interfered with the hijackers' attempt. The world watched through tear filled eyes and tried to grasp the complexity and horror of it all. Thousands died in New York and watching the building crumble was a sight that I will never forget. I still cry when I think of the terror all those people experienced. How awful for the poor passengers on the planes and those who died at the Pentagon.

Now, we are told that numerous other intended terrorist attacks were stopped that day and our government intelligence sources speak of other targets worldwide. President Bush has proclaimed a "war on terrorism" and the nation is now on highest alert. The news bombards us with reports about other terrorist attack strategies, including chemical and biological weapons. People are afraid to fly and Reagan International Airport in DC is still shut down. We have military in the Persian Gulf and numerous reservists are being deployed into active duty.

Here at home our first and most immediate concern is for Adam and how he might be called upon to serve. He went to Army boot camp this summer and spent eight weeks in Missouri. He described the experience as very difficult both emotionally and physically, but that he had learned a lot. I know he was very proud of his accomplishment. I flew out for his graduation and it was so special being able to be there. With Adam back home now, he is reporting to his National Guard battalion in Gardiner and his officers have told him that he will not be deployed while he is still in high school even if his unit is called to serve. That is certainly reassuring, but I can't help wondering if we knew six months ago what we know now, whether we would have signed the papers permitting Adam to join the Guard. He did it to help pay for his college tuition and was o.k. with serving for the State of Maine, but we never dreamed that something like this might require him to go off to war. I thought the National Guard did things like help in natural disasters and help secure the states. The recruiter had told us that the possibility of deployment was highly unlikely and that they would never pull him out of school or college to go, but now, I just don't know.

With the events of 9/11, this weighs heavily on all our minds. Last month at Donna's house we had a 9/11 Tribute Bunko and all the game money that we paid in to play was donated to the 9/11 fund for the families of those killed. We all dressed in red, white and blue and took up extra donations to be added to our usual Bunko dues. It was the least that we could do in a time when nothing seems enough.

Our ordinary little world continued on, of course, but never in isolation of all that happened around us. We stood by each other through the sorrows and the joys.

⋇

As a cool September breeze blew across the deck and rustled the leaves of the old dogwood tree, Auma stood stiffly. "Time to stretch my legs, my dear." Gingerly she picked up the half empty coffee cups and began to walk into the house. "These old bones can only sit for so long," she said as she winked and smiled. "Besides, I have something to show you. I'm pretty sure I can find it."

Emma rose and picked up the pan of cinnamon rolls as she followed her grandmother into the house. Auma rummaged through some photo albums on the shelf and finally came across the one labeled 2001. Auma was always so organized that way. All her albums were neatly labeled with the appropriate year and filed in order on her bookshelves. A life's worth of photos captured eighty years of memories.

She came back with a maroon colored album and when she thumbed through the pages, she found the picture taken in front of the World Trade Center. In between each letter spelling out "Peace on Earth" stood each of her friends. They were all in the picture. All except Auma. She was the person behind the camera. Most of her photos were like that because she was usually the photographer, but Emma found that thought provoking. Each photo was like seeing the world through Auma's eyes and over the years, those eyes had seen so much.

As they flipped through the pages of the album, the sound of the bulkhead door could be heard opening. Grampie Jake's heavy footsteps bounded up the cellar steps. "Are you two still at it? Don't let your grandmother bore you, Emma," Grampie said as he kissed Auma on the cheek and grabbed a cinnamon bun on his way out the back door.

"Do you have to get yourself home?" Auma asked.

"I don't have to be anywhere until the afternoon, so if you feel up to it, I'd like to stay a bit longer," Emma replied.

"Of course, honey! I love having you here. Let's sit in the living room, though. I was feeling a little chilled outside," Auma said as she grabbed her sweater from the chair and made her way toward the couch. With an all knowing smile and a nudge of her elbow, Auma said, "I wonder what happened next?"

Chapter Six
In Search of Peace

January 1, 2005

A new year. A better one I hope. I'm such a sucky journal writer. Time marches on and I write sporadically. I write when I'm provoked or challenged. And much like prayer, I pour out my inner soul in hope of finding truth. Truth within myself. Answers to my questions. Meaning from chaos. When at some point my children read this or other journals I've kept, they will realize that either their mother was a genius or a lunatic. That's up for debate. Even among the voices in my head that drive my pen. And no. Not voices like I'm schizophrenic, for God's sake; more like the voices of conscience, good vs. evil, right vs. wrong, strength vs. weakness. And through it all, I try to find balance. I hold out hope that this year will bring me peace. Peace of mind.

In spite of big issues happening all around us, our foolishness continued to keep the Society sane. For more years than any of us could count, we had been queens in our own right. We were all strong women who reigned in our private kingdoms with dignity and grace. But it was not until that day in September 2002 that Maggie decided to take the notion of "Queen" to new heights and came up with a plan to crown the first official Society of Sisters Queen. Every September, it was Maggie's turn to host Bunko, so that year Maggie bought a beautiful "jewel" encrusted crown, chose the first royal color of purple and talked Dale into sewing a royal sash. She even had an official "S.O.S. Queen of the Year" trophy made up at the local sporting goods store. I think the sales lady there thought she was nuts, but after a couple of years of Maggie doing this, she finally got on board and seemed to look forward to Maggie's annual trophy purchase.

Maggie decided that following our regular Bunko game we would have our First Annual Bunko Rolloff to determine which lucky Sister would be crowned Queen for the year. There was no real strategy or skill or even campaigning in the quest to be Queen. We didn't vote and it wasn't based on who deserved the crown that year. It was all literally just a crapshoot, a random roll of the dice. And by Society logic, what better means could we possibly use to determine such a high honor? Since in our game rolling three of a particular number is a Bunko, for that first Rolloff, Maggie chose a random number and whichever Sister was first to roll three of a kind of that number would be crowned Queen! It was quickly decided that once you were crowned a Queen, you would not be eligible to be Queen again until all the other Sisters had their turn to be Queen – so realistically you could be waiting around for over a decade before the honor came your way. "Away" Sisters were exempt from being crowned, as you needed to be present for fate to choose you in the Rolloff. That first year, our dear, sweet

Noelle was crowned and so began our annual coronation tradition.

Being Queen brought with it many perks. As Queen you had your choice of beds when we went away on a trip. You always got the number one placement at the head table when we played Bunko, and other Sisters would shower you with "suck up" gifts throughout the year. In turn, it was your royal obligation to decree fun, silly, or sometimes serious things for the Society of Sisters to do. Throughout the years Queens issued a wide variety of decrees, from the planting of favorite flowers in all the Sisters' gardens, to making the most creative snowman, to gathering to drink coffee on the beach at sunset. Sometimes Queens commanded that we take part in community related projects like donating items to soldiers overseas, putting together a Thanksgiving basket for a family in need, volunteering at a local food pantry, or walking in the Relay for Life. Each Queen reigned in her own way and according to her own style. Some, like Lynn, were flamboyant Queens who wore their crown and sash publicly and reveled in the power. Others like Noelle and Trudy were more subtle and reserved in their reigns, but no matter who was Queen, this new aspect of being one of the Society added to the excitement of it all. I loved my reign. I was third to be crowned and my royal color was blue. Good times, good times. There were years when I wondered if perhaps a catfight would ensue between certain Sisters in their yearning desire to be Queen. One person who shall remain anonymous (Maggie) thought for sure she was destined to be Queen the year our royal color was lime green. Boy, was she surprised and disappointed when Charlene cast a spell on the dice and rolled three fives right away. Too funny! In the end, of course, we all had our chance to be Queen. Even our families recognized our royal reigns. They thought we were insane, but they still went along with it all. They would joke among themselves about whose mom or wife was the best Queen. It was good to be the Queen.

The year I turned forty was the year that the Sisters ventured out again on another adventure together. I was determined to visit the magical city of New Orleans and it was wonderful that so many of my friends were on board with this trip. So, for many months, travel books were read, arrangements were made and all of us focused on saving up for our trip to the Big Easy.

What made me want to go to New Orleans, I can't say for sure, but it was as though something was drawing me there. The beauty of the French Quarter and magnificence of the Garden District were things I longed to see with my own eyes. There seemed to be such magic and mystery in the Crescent City. It was intriguing to think about having a psychic reading in a place where people are known to be in tune with that sort of thing and, while I still wasn't completely sure about what I believed, I was certainly curious.

On a bright day in early May we boarded a plane, all ten of us, and embarked on our first airborne S.O.S. adventure. We were not going during Mardi Gras – that may have been a bit too much fun even for us – but we were happy to be getting away from our cool Maine spring to a warmer climate. Queen Lynn made a point of wearing her crown on the plane and talked to everyone she saw about how she was Queen of the Society of Sisters. We had brought our little Bunko Barbie figurine with us as a mascot of sorts and the lucky flight attendant got to hear all about our plans for Queen Lynn and Barbie in New Orleans. I'm sure she thought we were nuts, but we didn't care. The great thing about New Orleans is that not even ten pale women from Maine carrying a tiny Barbie look out of place. It is a city that welcomes everyone and parties with them all.

Our hotel was an old establishment one block from Bourbon Street with a beautiful courtyard and balconied rooms. When we arrived, it was everything that I had hoped for. I don't really know what the others expected, but I think they were pleased. Once again, as the S.O.S. tour guide, I had lists of things for us to see during our four days. We wandered the streets and shops of the French Quarter, stopping at Café Du Monde for a beignet, then making our way to the waterfront where we took a short steamboat ride down the Mississippi. We gambled at Harrah's, drank Hurricanes at Pat O'Brien's, and ordered the famous New Orleans' sandwich – the muffuletta. Some of us went on a guided nighttime Haunted Tour where we heard the history of ghost sightings in the French Quarter, and we took the trolley all through the Garden District to see the old beautiful southern mansions. I can still envision the trees glistening in the sunlight from all the beads caught among their branches, hanging in silent tribute to the revelry of Mardi Gras just a couple of months before. At Preservation Hall we crammed all ten of us (and about fifty other people it seemed) into a tiny, little claustrophobic room in the sweltering humidity of a New Orleans evening to listen to real old time jazz played by old time jazz musicians. We drank "big ass beers" from "go cups" and sang bad karaoke until the wee hours of the morning. And of course, New Orleans wouldn't be New Orleans without earning a few beads of our own along the way. Despite the smell (which my friends called swill) that perfumes Bourbon Street when the heat of the day mixes with the stench of too much partying the night before, I loved that city. It was all that I hoped it would be. What a wonderful gift to commemorate my fortieth birthday and share another life memory with my best friends.

Before we left, I did have the opportunity to have a psychic reading done by an old shaman in the square by St. Louis Cathedral. This old weathered black man with a tall hat and kind wrinkles was not your everyday street "reader". He was an incense-sprinkling, bell-ringing, mumbo-jumbo type of mystic who seemed to be the perfect choice if I wanted to be "read" in New Orleans. His words have stayed with me a lifetime.

May 5, 2003

It is the last day of our trip and I don't have much time to write before we get ready to go out to dinner. A few of us went back down to the square by the Cathedral this afternoon in hopes that I might find someone to do a reading before we head back home tomorrow. After watching many other people's readings, I was drawn to this elderly black man who was theatrical in manner, but genuine in his presentation and, for whatever reason, he just seemed the most authentic person there. As I sat down, I didn't tell him anything about myself, he just began to talk to me. He described me as being on a journey and learning to be true to myself. He said that this was not always the case for me and that for many years I felt guilty for not being perfect. He told me to "fuck guilt". I thought that was non-conventional, but then, he was non-conventional. How true! Fuck guilt. The Shaman instructed me to buy a yellow candle and to light it every night and that this would bring me peace. I didn't know what that really meant, but I went on listening. As he closed his eyes, he told me that he saw me as living a long time, into my 80's; he thought 84 and said that someday we would meet again, but at that time I would help him instead. Then he said that I would go to Sedona and that this would be an important place for me – that the spirits are strong within me and I had a lot more work to do. He let me know that he was but one of my guides. As he finished, he told me to leave and go toward the river to look for a large sculpture. When I found the sculpture I was to meditate on it and I would find the answer that I seek. Before I left, he wrote down the titles of some books that he suggested I read, dusted me with incense, rang a little chime bell and then sent me on my way.

I didn't really know what to make of him, but thought that I should at least do as he said, so Lynn, Noelle, Dale and I walked along the river front until we saw a large silver chrome sculpture. I sat in the middle of it and waited. After a short time, the word balance kept ringing in my head. Balance. The sculpture meant balance. I need to find balance. I told the girls what came to me and we all left feeling like somehow we had experienced something bigger than ourselves. On the way back to the hotel, I stopped and bought a yellow candle too. And Sedona…what is Sedona?

Got to go, time to get in the shower before dinner. Balance. Aummmm. . .

Back home, with the war in Iraq continuing and no real end in sight, it was not surprising to get the phone call that every mother dreads. Adam had graduated from high school the year before and was finally enrolled at the University of Maine in Orono. He'd spent another summer and fall at Ft. Leonard Wood in Missouri to work on his advanced combat engineer training in which he had specialized as a combat engineer for the Army. After being away for a few months, he had returned to Maine to rejoin with his National Guard battalion in Gardiner, while beginning his freshman year a semester later than the rest of his friends. For months we wondered if he would be called upon to serve. So many of the National Guard were being deployed, but we kept hoping, given his enrollment as a college student, that they wouldn't pull him out of school to go. We clung to the hope that the recruiter had told us the truth, but I think recruiters tell you what you want to hear.

The morning of November 11th (Veterans Day – I find that ironic), Adam called to tell me that he had gotten his deployment papers. He would be shipping out within a month to go to Iraq and would be leaving UMO to come home shortly. I think I literally dropped the phone when he gave me the news. My whole body began to tremble, but as I tried to compose myself, I heard the voice of my twenty-year-old son consoling me. "Don't worry Mom, it will be o.k. I'm going with a really good group of guys and I trust them. We'll be o.k. I feel proud that we are doing this. Not everyone my age gets to have an experience like this." How brave he was - far braver than I. It's not fair! I don't want him to go! My Adam. . . my precious, precious Adam. As I hung up the phone, I needed to lean on a friend and the first person that I called that morning after my mom was Maggie. The shock that Adam was really being sent overseas had not sunk in and Maggie and I were both crying on the phone. My heart felt as though it was ripped apart, but I was thankful to have Maggie to share it with. What neither of us knew, however, was that this very day would rock our world in ways far greater than Adam's deployment.

Around two that afternoon, Maggie's husband Tom called me. His voice quivered as he tried to calmly tell me the unthinkable. Maggie was in the hospital and she had suffered a brain aneurysm! Shortly after my conversation with her that morning, she had begun to have a headache that rapidly grew to monumental proportions. Maggie had suffered with migraines for years, but this was far worse than her worst migraine. She could barely walk as Tom got her into the car and took her to a nearby hospital. When she arrived at the small local hospital the emergency room staff realized pretty quickly that they were not equipped to handle something like this and transferred her to a mid-sized hospital nearby. Tom asked me to let the other Sisters know what was happening and, while he didn't ask me to, I told him that Audri and I would be coming right over. Oh, my God! Maggie, one of my best friends in the whole world, was all of a sudden in this life and death situation – it seemed so surreal as we had just spoken a few hours earlier. At first I wondered if my news could given her such shock that it caused her aneurysm, but when I picked Audri up to drive to the hospital, she assured me that this could not be the case. I'm sure that she must be right, but sometimes I still wonder.

When we arrived at the hospital, Maggie was in ICU and had been diagnosed with a level four brain bleed. While I had never known anything about aneurysms, I realized immediately that Maggie was in grave danger. Tom seemed relieved to see us and happy to have the added support. Audri and I sat in the waiting room with Tom, Maggie's parents and her friend Ellie. We listened intently as the doctor told us that he planned to wait until the next morning to do an operation on Maggie's brain in which he would surgically seal off the aneurysm with a clip. The greatest difficulty was in how much blood was now seeping into the brain as this could cause damage that sometimes cannot be repaired.

As we listened to the doctor, the family all seemed to be dazed by his words and understandably overwhelmed by it all. I spoke up and asked the doctor how many of these surgeries he had done. When he admitted not many, Audri and Ellie, both of whom are nurses, began to question the capability of the hospital to handle this type of surgery and asked questions about the variety of procedures available. As we sat there in this big circle, we were faced with determining the fate of what was to happen with Maggie. I remember feeling very uncomfortable with the situation, and debating whether or not I should speak up. It seemed that the family was agreeing with this doctor's plan and that worried me greatly. Finally, I got up the nerve to open my mouth. I told Tom and Maggie's parents that although I was not a member of their family and it was certainly their decision, I loved Maggie like a sister and I wouldn't be able to live with myself if they didn't consider getting Maggie to a larger hospital that specialized in neurosurgery. We were talking about BRAIN surgery here, not some random common place procedure.

It is so hard for families when they are suddenly faced with making these decisions and the doctors are talking as if they are all experts. After my own experience, I knew firsthand that when you have something seriously wrong, you seek a specialist. My brother-in-law was the one who pushed us in that direction and indirectly saved my life, and now it was my turn. Maggie's brain was bleeding and I knew that there could be irreparable damage. Would she survive the procedure and even if she did, would she have impairment cognitively, with speech and language or motor response? I felt like I went out on a limb that day, saying what I did when perhaps it was not my place, but knowing what I know now, I thank God that I did.

Maggie's friend Ellie called a neurologist that she knew and got the name of a world-renowned specialist in the field of neurosurgery in Boston. With that, Tom knew he had the support he needed to arrange transport that evening for Maggie from the local hospital to Mass General in Boston. As it turned out, Maggie began to bleed more on the ambulance ride down and we were told later that, had she not been moved when she was, she would certainly have died! As we entered the ICU one by one to see her that afternoon, I didn't know if she would pull through it all. I held her hand and told her I loved her. Perhaps this was how people felt when they came to see me. I don't know, but I didn't like being on the other side of the situation. I still cry when I picture her lying there. I would choose to have cancer again rather than see someone I love go through what Maggie did. But looking back on that time, I sometimes smile at how inexplicable life really is. Had I not lived through my cancer, I wouldn't have been there to say what I did in the waiting room that day and Maggie's family might have not taken the steps to get her the cutting edge care she needed. Her surgeon saved her life, but in a way, so did her friends.

The operation at Mass General was a success and miraculously, Maggie came through with flying colors. I went down to see her a few times in the ICU that week and was so relieved to know that she survived her procedure. Prior to the surgery, Maggie had beautiful, long, flowing brown hair, a feature she was very proud of, and so when I saw her with a large shaved spot on her right temple, I worried how she would handle it. But in those first days, she really didn't know or care what she looked like. The surgery had gone well and the clip had been put in. A stent had also been placed in her head and liquid continually flushed her brain to help alleviate swelling. I'm certainly not up on all the specifics of aneurysms, but I do know that for days following surgery, they closely monitored Maggie's every level.

Because she was in ICU it was impossible for all her Sisters to visit and so I was their spokesperson. Dale made Maggie a beautiful blanket with individually designed hands all over it in symbolism of all of us there hugging her. Tom and their kids, Elaine and Mike, seemed to be doing quite well and holding it together. Families are often quiet about their feelings when something of this magnitude happens; I know that's how it was with my kids when I was sick. Elaine and Mike knew how serious this had been, but were focusing on their mom's recovery, which is as it should be.

After a little over a week, Maggie was released from the hospital and was so happy to be home. We were all amazed that, in spite of the danger she was in and the amount of cerebral bleeding that she had suffered, Maggie emerged free of any complications. She had all of her thoughts and memories intact. She had no difficulty with communicating and had no loss of gross or fine motor skills. The only thing that she was left to deal with was a very bad haircut, but after an ordeal like the one she had been through, hair was an insignificant thing. She cut it all very short and wore a fabulous "Survivor" baseball cap. Maggie was always into reality TV and now, she had certainly earned the role of sole Survivor!

Maggie's crisis had for a time diverted my attention away from Adam's upcoming deployment. However, with her recovery well under way, I was again faced with the inevitable. Initially, Adam was to be shipped before Christmas to Ft. Drum in New York for training, and then sent overseas soon thereafter, but we were all very thankful to hear that the battalion commander had been able to change the arrangements and keep his soldiers home through Christmas. Adam left UMO without finishing the semester, which was unfortunate, but we were just so happy to have a little more time with him. The holidays passed and the day when we would finally be faced with saying goodbye was approaching. He was going for an eighteen-month deployment and, while we didn't know the exact location of where he'd be stationed, we did know that he was going to Iraq.

January 6, 2004

How does a mother send her son off to a war-torn place with nothing but uncertainty of what lies ahead? It's just not natural. As mothers, we cry when they get on the school bus for kindergarten, cry when they achieve their first soccer goal or home run, cry when they go to the prom, and cry when we leave them at college for the first time. Even with this understanding, watching your son drive away in his Army convoy is a feeling that defies words. As you stand there in the cold morning air, you feel immense pride for the man he has become and at the same time the immense loss of the little boy he once was. You don't ever stop being a mom and in that moment, when the trucks drive down the road, past the fanfare of well-wishers, your heart is breaking, because he's still your baby and he'll be gone and in harm's way for a long time. Thousands, even millions, of mothers have sent their sons to war. It's an ageless event that has been happening almost as long as time itself, and yet I never gave it much thought. Until today. Today Adam left to go to Iraq.

After the good-byes and tears and after the convoy pulled away, we drove back to Phillipstown. We saw Adam on the highway. There he was behind the wheel of his big truck - fourth in the procession of trucks. We waved again and when he beeped, I cried. I cried all the way home, actually. And pretty much all morning and into the afternoon. Gut wrenching sobs that left me nauseous and at times took my breath away. It may sound excessive, but, honest to God, I couldn't control it. He is gone and 18 months seems like an eternity.

Finally by 2 p.m. I figured it was time to confront the day and focus. I don't like crying and I don't like losing control. I called Lynn to come over and get me out of the house. It sounds ridiculous to most people, I'm sure, but we have these big coats. Big, gigantic fur coats that are ridiculously funny, but we call them our "comfort coats" and today they were needed. We sat in Lynn's van, wrapped in fur, drinking Dunkin' Donut's coffee and looking out over the town's pond. Crying and talking and me eating a chocolate donut ('cause it was a chocolate sort of day), but Lynn stuck with coffee 'cause she was doing the Atkins diet thing. Another new year. Another resolution. As the afternoon sky began to darken, we watched the full moon, thinking that Adam was looking up at the same moon. It's a comforting thought and I held on to that. I can't help smiling to myself when I think of us there, in the moonlight, in our ridiculous coats. And what else were we to do given the circumstances? How often do you send your son into a war conflict? We called Audri, Maggie and Trudy (but Trudy was not home). We told them to find their coats and meet at Audri's house. Lynn and I brought yellow ribbon and were determined to tie it to an old oak tree. Audri had the perfect tree and so it goes...by the time we got together, I'd used up all my tears, but the camaraderie of 4 grown women wearing fur coats, tying a ribbon to an old oak tree on a cold moonlit night made perfect sense and helped me feel a little better. It's been a weird day. . . one I couldn't have imagined even if I tried.

With Adam at Fort Drum waiting to be shipped out, I desperately needed a diversion and, thankfully, Audri was about to celebrate her fiftieth birthday, so we had the perfect excuse to throw a party. Now, anyone who knew Audri also knew that she wanted a party. It wasn't every day that Audri turned the big 5-0. But, we also knew that it would be hard for her husband to plan it, so I called him up and told him that the Sisters would take care of planning it for him. Although Maggie was only two months into her recovery time, she too was happy to have a project to focus on and volunteered the use of her house for this event. Lynn, Maggie and I had some serious planning to do in order to pull off a surprise that would impress Audri.

Audri, of all our friends, has class. She enjoys the finer things in life and often jokes that, while she loves her husband, she should have married for money. With Audri in mind, style was what it was all about, so we decided to throw a lavish resort-theme party. We went all out, decorating Maggie's great room with a canopy of sheer fabric cascading from the vaulted ceiling to give the effect of a luxurious spa. Mini white lights were everywhere and plants and fountains adorned the furniture. A glass top patio table with raised stools became a martini bar, complete with our own original drink that we named the Audri-tini in the birthday girl's honor.

Maggie's dining room was transformed into the resort's "Club Audri". The furniture was all removed and rope lighting outlined the dance floor, while neon martini lamps added a soft blue glimmer. Charlene, ever our gifted artist, made wonderful signs and the words "Club Audri" leaped out in gold and silver glitter. With Audri's husband footing the bill, we planned a wonderful menu and stocked enough alcohol to create Audri-tinis for all!

On the evening of the big event, the Society of Sisters arrived in our signature black outfits, each reflecting our own personal style. We knew that there would be many photo opportunities that evening. With everyone waiting silently in the great "spa" room, Audri's eldest daughter brought her to the party and when they opened the door, Audri's look of shock and awe made all the effort worthwhile! It was a great moment and, while the situation with Adam was certainly on our minds, we had our Maggie with us and we were thrilled to celebrate both Audri and the gift of our friendship that evening. With

Motown music flowing, the Sisters danced all night long while our husbands ate and mingled with each other. Life had brought us all together so long ago and, in spite of all that we had encountered, our friendship was what continued to help us get through.

February 22, 2004

Time has a way of moving on and life stops for no one. Adam has been at Fort Drum for nearly 2 months now and has spent time in the cold frigid weather practicing maneuvers and learning to say "Stop or I'll shoot" in Iraqi. What kind of world do we live in and where is the sanity in all that is happening? Adam has been able to call us quite a bit and for that I'm thankful. It will be different when he gets where he is going. Every call is a moment of connection with the son that I love. He sounds like he is next door or maybe up at Orono and I pretend that he is. He's up at Orono with his friends where he belongs... and yet I know it's all a farce. He's at Ft. Drum dressed in Army fatigues, practicing war maneuvers and learning to handle land mines. He leaves this week. Wednesday to be exact, but we are not really supposed to know. All is secret when it comes to war. Granted, this is no longer considered "war" – just a "war zone" according to stupid President Bush. Send his twins there and I bet he'll think it's war. I hate it. My child is getting sent to some hostile environment where people hate Americans and where loyalists try and kill our soldiers and supporters. And yet, he is proud of the work he's about to do. Rebuilding the country for the people. I know this boy, my son, this man wants to make his mark in history. How can I not be proud? My heart aches for him – so proud and yet so afraid for all that he is about to embark upon.

February 25, 2004

Adam's on the plane. He left this afternoon sometime and said that it will be a 15½ hour plane ride, so I imagine he is still in the air. He called last night and while it was great to hear his voice, I felt so sad having to say goodbye again. I shouldn't have cried. I didn't want him to be more upset than need be and I was upset at myself for letting my guard down like that. I need to be strong for him, as he is for me. I just pray that he'll be safe and arrive without incident wherever he is going. He didn't know exactly – maybe Kuwait or maybe directly to Mosul. I can't believe that this day has finally come and he is really gone. God, watch over him while he is away.

With Adam away, things at home continued as they do. Jake and I were doing well as far as our relationship went. I loved Jake. No question about that. He brought to our relationship a strength that I hadn't known with Chris, but it was more of a personal strength rather then a financial one. Jake was a guy's guy. He mowed the lawn, tinkered in the garage, wouldn't let me touch a snow shovel and took care of all the "manly" chores. He helped out with laundry, too, so it wasn't all one-sided. Football season was his favorite "holiday". Strong and silent, he wasn't a huge conversationalist, but I had all my Sisters for that. With Jake, the years brought a subtle magic that remained with us always.

In spite of our continued connection, Jake had his ups and downs career wise though. In the eight years that I'd known him, he'd changed jobs four times and periodically been out of work for months in between. I loved Jake for who he was, not what he did. With my job at the school department to rely on, I appreciated knowing that, in spite of it all, we were able to stay financially afloat. It is funny, because looking back on that time, I often wonder how we did all that we did. We managed to take a number of vacation trips with the kids to build family memories and we put in a beautiful swimming pool, but realistically, while it might have appeared to people that we "had money," we really didn't. Our middle class income went from years with two medium range incomes to just having mine, and we saw pay ranges that jumped $40,000 at a time. Fortunately even on just my salary, we lived more or less within our means. I had huge school loans, but our mortgage was very low, and we drove two ten-year-old vehicles with little or no payments. We did carry some credit card debt from the trips and we had a relatively small home equity loan on the pool, but through it all, we were frugal. I was the queen of bargain shopping and had always been excellent at saving money at the grocery store. So, while "vacation" had been a part of our budget in the years Jake was working, we were still able to get by during the times he wasn't. I sort of liked knowing that I could handle things financially, but always hoped that someday Jake would find the right job. One that he liked and that he could really invest in. Money never mattered to me; I just wanted him to be happy.

Elizabeth was a junior in high school by this time and much of my energy was used up in worrying about her. My Elizabeth. . . while her younger years had certainly held moments of being strong-willed, being a teenager brought it all to new heights. At times the social drama that had unraveled since junior high school was like traveling on a psychotic roller coaster ride of emotionality. It's not as though Adam had been a saint or anything, but boys are different. They don't get sucked into all the emotional baloney that girls seem to deal with. He did stupid things like blowing out the windshield of his car by playing his rap music too loud and getting pulled over once for speeding, but he didn't have any drama. He had a steady girlfriend and, while I know he partied a bit, it never seemed like it got out of control.

Young girls, however, were ruthless. One minute they would all be friends and then the next minute they would be talking behind each other's backs on the Internet on something called ICQ chat rooms. While Elizabeth's grades were always good, all the school drama was really difficult. As she entered high school, her group of friends remained intact and although initially I thought most of the kids were "good kids", I learned that even good kids do bad things and make bad decisions. When Elizabeth said that she would be at her friend Sarah's house, I would go to Sarah's at midnight to find that she was not really there. She and her friends seemed to get caught every time, but in spite of consequences, they didn't seem to learn their lesson. I think some kids are just like that. They have to learn from experience and while that does not make it easy on them or their parents, it just is a fact. As much as you try to tell them or guide them, they have to go through it themselves.

With Adam away, Elizabeth seemed to calm down a little during the months that followed his deployment and she spent a fair amount of time at home. I was hoping that we were reconnecting and that this would improve things. In reality, it was just a short reprieve, but it was nice while it lasted. By the time junior prom came that spring, I was so excited to think that I had lived long enough to see her attend prom. Back when I was sick, it was one of the things I hoped I'd live to see. But, with Jake out of work, I wondered how we would afford the prom dress. Prom is a big deal in Phillipstown. The gowns are exquisite, the girls get their hair and nails done, and kids rent limos to deliver them to the prom. I told Elizabeth from the start that I had a limited budget and that we would have to shop at the mall rather than the bridal stores where the other girls were shopping. She really was very good about that. She hadn't fussed or anything, but I knew in my heart that she loved this pale blue, beaded Cinderella-type dress she had seen at a shop in town. Lynn's daughter Jessica was also going to the prom that year and had her eye on a pink strapless gown fit for a princess.

One Saturday, Lynn had called me up to see if I wanted to go looking at prom dresses. We went to the store where both dresses were sold. Knowing Jake was out of work again, recognizing my worry for Adam, and remembering my dream when I was sick of seeing Elizabeth at prom, Lynn bought Elizabeth her dream dress that day. Lynn and I had carried our girls at the same time and raised our two daughters together, and here we were, seventeen years later, sharing the prom experience together. Elizabeth never knew that Lynn was really the one who bought that dress, as Lynn made me promise not to tell, but I can tell the truth now. I don't know if Lynn really knew how much that meant to me. It was such a special gift and one that I have never, ever forgotten. Once again, a Sister made another imprint on my heart.

April 16, 2004

It is up to a wife or mother to be the backbone of our family. If we let ourselves fall apart, our families and husbands begin to question themselves and slip backward into places too scary to enter. But, when we women hold strong, we are able to empower those around us. Husbands and work, sons and deployment, daughters and high school. It all rests on us. We kid ourselves if we think otherwise. There are moments when I fall into the abyss of emotional instability – plummet into the deepest black hole imaginable – and so often only another woman can pull me out. Women understand the black hole and the despair that it holds. I've been in that hole. A place too dark for words. And then like a gift, shopping for prom dresses provides a mini reprieve. Why on earth a sparkly impractical dress matters, I have no idea, and yet it does. Control. It all comes back to control. The control that I no longer have. And me, the control freak. I am. I know it. This is a test. The proverbial rug is being pulled out from under me taking away all illusion of control. Elizabeth is in high school. Partying. Doing whatever she is doing. No control. Adam is off in a hostile land. No control. Jake is out of work. No control. I only control my own destiny and my own choices. Not theirs. I pray that God will watch over them all and give me the strength to support – not control. For there is no more control. And I'm o.k. with that...or at least I'm learning to be. It is a hard lesson.

The summer arrived and Jake finally got a job working for the town. He really seemed to be happy there and I was hopeful that perhaps this would be the right match for him. I counted the months till Adam's return. I sent care packages to him every week and sometimes sent packages for his friends too. They were stationed in Mosul, Iraq and were doing a lot of rebuilding in that area. His unit mostly did survey work, but also rebuilt roads, sidewalks and airports. They spent a lot of time doing concrete work. In between his projects, he also spent time on guard duty securing the perimeter of the base that they had set up at Camp Marez. Overall, he sounded good when he called and his spirits seemed to be high, in spite of missing home. It was nice to know that he had made such strong connections with all the men with whom he was serving.

Earlier in the spring, a young man in his unit had been killed in a roadside attack. His death hit home very hard - his was a face that I'd seen and I could remember his foreign wife who sat across from us at the send-off meeting, asking many questions. My heart ached for her and his family. His death brought home the fact that, although Adam seemed in good spirits, the possibility of tragedy lurked around every corner. I went to a memorial service that the battalion had for the soldier and as we all stood in a large circle, one by one we lit a yellow candle for our own soldier's safety. As we all stood side by side and cried, I was brought back to my Shaman's words. . . a yellow candle. . . he told me that a yellow candle would bring me peace.

Back at home, all we could do was to take things one day at a time and focus on the little we could do to make a difference. I started a Parents of Soldiers support group and sold magnetic car ribbons that said "Pray for our Troops". With the help of Portland radio station The Coast 93.1 and D.J. Tim Wright, we collected "CDs for GIs". Over a 1,000 CDs were donated to be shipped to our two Maine battalions serving in Iraq. The Sisters did their part, too, by putting together care packages and donating money to help with all the shipping. Most importantly, they remained my sounding board and helped me keep my sanity in an insane time.

July 20, 2004

I'm at my wit's end. The summer of Hell. I'm worried for Adam and I'm equally worried for Elizabeth. She is sucked into a bad crowd. Even her friends are doing bad things - partying too much and the people they are hanging out with are really scary. I don't blame them though. She is making her own choices. She is dating some boy named Evan who literally has a police record. The more we tell her not to see him, the more she does anyway. We have spent all summer worrying 24/7 about her. We've had calls from the Old Orchard Police Dept. regarding a fight that broke out and an intoxication incident. She was not in the fight, but she was at the scene. I can't even begin to describe this Hell. Once again my life feels totally out of control. A continuing theme it seems. I cannot control things. And with my children coming of age, there is certainly no controlling them. But I really don't want to control her, only protect her. Elizabeth's mistakes have to be her own, but I continue to pray that she live through them. Maggie's advice continues to ring through my head. . . "This too shall pass."

August 8, 2004

She tried to run away last night! Why is she doing this to me? I know that it's not really "to me", but it feels that way. In a million years, I would never have guessed that my child would act this way. She has such a wonderful side to her, but I'm feeling like I'm losing her. She wants independence. I want her to be safe.

The day didn't start out that way. A few of the girls were over yesterday afternoon – we were sitting on the back deck visiting together. Elizabeth called me into the house and tells me that she is going to Evan's house. I tell her no because I don't want her there – I know what they do over there, smoking pot and drinking. He's not a good influence on her! I'm screaming at her, she's screaming at me, I take her car keys – total power struggle – and my friends are sitting on the back deck hearing the chaos. Audri tried to calm me down and told me that I shouldn't be screaming hysterically. I was making it worse, which I was. Trudy tried to talk to me and reassure me that things would be o.k. Lynn and Maggie tried to talk to Elizabeth and calm her down. I was hoping that maybe they'd talk some sense into her. But no, Elizabeth ended up running upstairs, slamming the door of her bedroom and screaming that she hates me. Meanwhile, I was crying and I went back outside to sit with the girls. They are all here for me and I know that. I didn't like them to see what was going on, though. As much as Elizabeth was acting hateful, I didn't want them to judge her. Such a balancing act when you are the mom. Your kid is being incorrigible, but you still want to protect their dignity and your own.

But, the night was not over. Later that evening, in the midst of a torrential rainstorm, Elizabeth tells Jake and me that she is running away and we can't stop her! Evan is coming to get her *and she's leaving. We say, "You're not going anywhere with that boy. He has a suspended license." But, there she was, standing in the door with her bag packed and hatred for us all over her face. She stood there looking at us as if we were such horrible people for wanting to protect her. So, the cops get called. She is running out in the rain to meet Evan and he gets arrested in front of the house for driving without a valid license! Arrested! Blue lights and all! Unbelievable! So, this morning, after a night full of tears, I took Elizabeth to counseling with the Crisis Response people. She was willing to go. But there seem to be no good answers. They told me that if she wants to run away, at her age, we can't stop her! We should just call Crisis Response! She's my daughter whom I love! Why can't I protect her??? How did it come to this? Faith. That is all I have left to rely on. Faith that she will come through this and that she will be o.k. This is part of her journey and I suppose, part of mine.*

October brought the turning point that I prayed for. As scary as any car accident is, the morning that I got that call from Elizabeth was the first catalyst for change. Her life took a huge U-turn and inadvertently set her on a new and better path. She had been at Sarah's family's camp the night before. At about 7:00 that morning she was driving home and, being unfamiliar with the camp roads, she overshot a stop sign and got hit broadside by an SUV. Had her car been out another foot or so and she would have taken the full impact on her driver's side door. That type of hit could have killed her, but by the grace of God or the watchful eyes of a guardian angel (who I have always thought might have been her paternal grandfather), she came out of that accident without one scratch or bruise. Her car was totaled. Her two passengers, Sarah and a boy named Joe, seemed o.k. – maybe a bit bruised, but mostly just shook up. When Jake and I got to the scene, the officers were interrogating Elizabeth and asking if she had been drinking. While she had not had anything to drink that morning, she did admit to drinking the night before and so, because she was eighteen and underage, they put her in a police car and took her off to the station. Her blood point alcohol level was well below the legal limit and so, thankfully, she was released, but the experience still had its impact on her. She ended up losing her license for a month for the stop sign infraction, but she didn't actually drive for over six months because she didn't have a vehicle. Ironically, to top it all off, her "best" friend Sarah blamed her for the accident and their friendship dissolved. I was so thankful that finally Elizabeth was able to distance herself from that group of people.

Elizabeth stopped seeing Evan and got a job at a local clothing store to try and save up money for a new car. In addition to paying for a new car, she knew that now she would be taking out her own insurance policy, as Jake and I said that we wouldn't cover her anymore. It was all a huge wake up call for Elizabeth. Not only did she lose her car, but her friends also turned their back on her. More importantly, she realized that she could have lost her life and now began to take responsibility for her actions. We found her a new counselor who connected well with her and ultimately diagnosed her with Attention Deficit Disorder. Perhaps that was some of the difficulty that she had struggled with throughout her life. We tried some new medication that really helped her in every way. She focused on finishing high school early to get away from that gang of kids and then enrolled in cosmetology school. With new goals to hold on to, Elizabeth became a new person. It was as though all the best things in my daughter came to the surface and all the potential that I knew she possessed finally came shining through. Perhaps as a parent, our worries create illusions of danger that take on monumental proportions and drive us to the brink of insanity. Yet it is our love that keeps us grounded in our quest to raise our children and see them through to adulthood in one piece. Lynn once told me, "The deeper the darkness, the more joy we find in the light." I was so thankful that one moment in time, one stop sign, one "accident" helped me find that joy and gave my beautiful Elizabeth back to me. I have always loved her so much!

Meanwhile, I wasn't the only Sister with teen issues. The other girls had their share of ups and downs, too. Lynn's youngest son continued to give her a run for her money. Liz's boys, who she playfully referred to as the "little bastards" in S.O.S. conversations, also kept her holding her breath until they finally made their way through high school. Our friends with younger kids knew that their time was coming. It wasn't really a question of "if", as much as "when". Very few of our children were totally exempt from the "terrible teens", but some certainly came through with more war stories than others. Thank God we had each other back then.

We were already earning our Auma name. Each day seemed to hold some drama or trauma. Like the camaraderie of raising toddlers, the fellowship of raising teens proved even more important. People with sweet little kids always think "my child would never do that" or "I would never allow my kid to do that". Ha. That is all I have to say. We were all great parents who loved our sons and daughters a hundred and ten percent of the time. We were the parents who went to parent conferences and coached the sports. We were totally involved. But, when the Peons got to be teens, as much as we all did our best to have good rules and hold the kids accountable, being a teen is about coming of age and breaking a rule now and then. And when the Peons did, the Sisters came to each other's emotional rescue.

December 1, 2004

The holidays are almost upon us and I can't believe how much I miss Adam. He was home briefly at the end of October for two weeks, which was wonderful, but sending him back was as hard as the first time. He looks good – thin, but very fit. There is a seriousness to him that he didn't have before, but his eyes still reflect my gentle boy. He had to leave on his 21st birthday of all days. . . and I kept thinking that it shouldn't be this way. He should be home celebrating with his friends. In spite of it all, he is taking one day at a time and that is a good thing. Here at home, my parents support group is making Christmas stockings for all the Maine troops and I am making personal stockings for Adam and all his best friends. I got a small tree at the dollar store and a bunch of decorations that I plan to mail out to him. I have two cartons of gifts for the boys - little things that I hope will make them smile. Putting that together is what is helping to make Christmas more bearable. It's weird. Doing things like that keep me going and make me feel that at least I am making a difference while he is there. Keeping busy is my only means of sanity. I have learned to stop watching the news. It's just too much for me. Sometimes I've felt responsible for him being there. I never should have allowed him to join the National Guard, but then again, that too was really out of my hands. And like the Shaman said, "Fuck guilt." Maybe this is a part of the journey that Adam is meant to take.

The insurgency has heated up over the past month or so and the battalion has moved Adam to the position of gunner on the convoy. I am out of my mind with worry. My entire day seems consumed with wondering what he is doing in that moment and questioning whether or not he is safe. Every day he is going out there, sitting high on his jeep with nothing but a metal shield in front of him and no protection from the side or behind. Their vehicles aren't even really combat prepared! The troops themselves have had to armor them up. It's just not right! We live in the richest country in the world and yet we send our sons and daughters into this God forsaken war with scrap metal to protect them! There is a huge machine gun mounted on the front of the jeep by the shield. He tells me that his vehicle is last in line and protects the convoy from the rear. He sent me a few pictures and tells me that, although he has fired his weapon and has been fired upon, he has never had to kill anyone. Not yet anyway. How awful! I keep thinking that again it is in God's hands. Perhaps there is a reason that he is on this new duty and I have to have faith that whatever is meant to be will be. I pray that God gives him the strength along the way and gives me the strength as a mom to do the right thing – whatever that is. It's my job to be strong for everyone else. When I waiver, they waver. When I'm o.k., they're o.k.

December 22, 2004

Yesterday was the most difficult day I have ever endured! Adam's Camp Marez was bombed – the mess hall was hit and two soldiers from the 133rd died! One was a boy that Adam went to boot camp with and the other was an older man in his unit. When we first got word, we knew that the mess tent was hit, but I had no way of knowing whether Adam was in there at the time of the attack. The Portland paper has been embedded with stories about the 133rd for the past month or so, and as soon as the attack happened, they reported on the story. The reporters mentioned Adam's sergeant by name as one who was in the mess tent and when I saw that, I was sure that Adam must have been there too. Jake and I waited by the phone all day long, knowing that he would certainly call to let us know he was o.k. as soon as he was able. We checked the battalion website for possible news, but as afternoon turned to evening, we were still without word. As vehicles drove down our street I was sure that one of them was the Chaplain coming to give us the dreaded news. Black SUVs with men in uniform scare me more than anything else. They haunt my dreams and worry me to the point of nausea. Finally we had word from the battalion that the families of those soldiers who had died had been notified. What mixed feelings came over me. . . relief to know that my son was still alive, but immense grief for the families of those lost. Somehow it all seemed so unfair and unnecessary and with just a few days before Christmas, it was beyond sad. We still did not know whether Adam was perhaps injured as many more hours passed. I waited up all night long. Finally, thank God, this morning he called to say that he was o.k. He had been off on a convoy when the bomb attack had happened and was not at camp at that time. How ironic, that the very thing I worried most about ended up saving him from being there. No other Christmas present matters; this was the very best gift that I could ever possibly receive!

Chapter Seven
Finding Balance

September 29, 2007

And me, I'm well. I celebrated my 8th survival anniversary today! At one time, I never knew whether or not I would get here and yet, here I am! I know there is still the slim chance that my cancer could return, but I'm more at peace with it now. I hold to my thought of balance. Balance is found in the breath of contentment. One day, one breath at a time. We should be content in the moment and this gets us past any difficulties we might encounter. It all seems manageable then. My cancer helped me begin the process of self-search and all the other experiences helped enhance it. I have come to believe that we all have the divine within us if only we open our hearts and minds to it. It's not about one people or one religion, it's about connection and humanity and the divinity inside. God speaks to us if we listen.

As winter turned to spring, hope was around the corner. Adam was scheduled to come home and we all anxiously awaited his homecoming. The Sisters and I got together to make posters and banners to welcome him and on that amazing day in early March, we waited together at the Portland Armory to see him march into the room with his battalion. All our family, along with friends, townspeople and members of the press came out that day to welcome our troops. As I stood at the front of the line, I strained to see through the sea of camouflage to find my boy. Red, white and blue balloons created a patriotic arch under which they marched in and all the spectators waved flags as they cheered. Finally our eyes met and I knew he was really home. After a final moment of military pageantry, the battalion commander gave the order to break formation and we all rushed to embrace our soldiers. Hugging Adam again and knowing that he had made it safely back to U.S. soil was a feeling that I can't possibly describe. We were so incredibly blessed and yet, while I was overwhelmed with personal relief for Adam, my heart ached knowing that not all of our Maine soldiers had come home.

May 1, 2005

Time has passed and Adam has gratefully returned to civilian life. He is very much of the opinion that he just wants his time over there to be done. He didn't attend the large parade in Portland and only participated in Phillipstown's acknowledgment ceremony after I asked him to. The town had been so supportive while he was away. I can understand, though, that he wants that chapter in his life closed. To the best of my knowledge he came home without many battle scars, physical or emotional. He doesn't really talk about it. He did tell me that he never had to kill anyone, but that he did see people die. In spite of that, he doesn't seem to be plagued with nightmares and thankfully, his only physical scars are cigarette burns on his hand. You'll have to ask him about that. Stupid macho military shit if you ask me. But none the less, he is back to his old life now and that is a blessing.

He's dating a new girl and spending lots of time with her. After being away all that time I know that he just wants "normalcy". As a mom it can be hard having sons. They spend all their time with the girlfriend's family. That is how Adam was in high school and it seems that it is the way he is again. Most guys are like that and I understand it. I accept it. What's the old saying about how a daughter is with you all of her life, but a son leaves when he takes a wife? Not exactly the wording, but you get my drift. It's true. I missed him so much all those months he was away and now I still miss him. But at least now I know he's safe. I can handle his absence. He is going to be renting a house with four of his friends up in Old Town and then he'll start his classes at the University of Maine again in September. I'm very thankful to have him back.

The National Guard awarded me a beautiful embroidered banner and a medal for my work helping the troops. That was very special to me and I appreciated the recognition.

Elizabeth graduated with honors from high school early last January but will go back to march with her class in June. It seems so strange. With Elizabeth attending her cosmetology school in Portland and usually off doing things with her new friends and Adam busy with his life, Jake and I are beginning to experience the whole "empty nest" thing. It's odd to think that we are already at that point in our lives. Elizabeth still officially lives with us, but is here so seldom, on many nights Jake and I are by ourselves. Sometimes I am sad to think that the kids are all grown up. I miss the days when we hung out as a family or did things with my friends like spending the day at the beach together. I miss the moments when their little arms would hug me and they'd say "I love you, Mommy." Being a mom has always been such an important part of who I am. It still is, but now I *suppose it takes on new meaning. It is all just another phase in our lives.*

With both my children safe and sound, the girls and I set our sights on another S.O.S. adventure. Our friend Ginger and her family had moved from Europe back to the United States and settled in Arizona of all places. With Ginger there already, it made perfect sense that we take the Shaman's advice and go visit Sedona. A plan emerged in which we would fly to Tucson, visit overnight with Ginger's family, then rent two cars (one being a convertible so that we could take turns traveling "Thelma and Louise" style) and drive north to Sedona where we would stay for three days. Once again, I took on the role of travel agent and had a great time learning about all the things that we might do while we were out west. I didn't know it originally, but soon learned that Sedona is known for its beautiful red rocks and its many mystical vortex meditation sites for those who believe in that sort of thing.

Literally the day after school was over for the summer, we boarded a plane and began our Western adventure. Ginger's house was a beautiful southwestern style home with a lovely pool and patio in the back yard. It was wonderful having the chance to visit with her family. In full S.O.S. style, we took over the house, donned cowboy hats and played poker until long after midnight. The next morning, we loaded up our rental cars and, with Ginger's car added to the caravan, we piled into the three vehicles and took to the road. Having never been to the West before, I was amazed by the landscape! The desert stretched for miles and tall cacti stood like solemn statues as far as the eye could see. On our way north, we met up with Donna's brother who lives outside of Phoenix. Like Donna, her family exudes a wonderful display of enthusiasm for life and when you are around them, their boisterous laughter is contagious! Together we all enjoyed a wonderful lunch at The Satisfied Frog. The restaurant had this tribute wall called "Crazy Ed's Tequila Wall of Fame" with small plaques commemorating individuals who had taken the Tequila Challenge – drinking ten tequila shots in one sitting. So, given that my mind was always scheming, I asked the waitress if we could take the Tequila Challenge as a group and get our name "The Society of Sisters" added to the wall. I don't really have to tell you what happened, because you already know the answer. Not everyone liked tequila, but we were always up for a challenge. Go visit the Satisfied Frog and you'll see that the Society were there!

Getting there is half the fun, at least according to Lynn, and she was all about being "funny", so the drive north was riddled with moments of tourist insanity and outdoor bathroom breaks, watching my friends squat over cacti and wondering if life would finally bite them in the ass. After all, there were a lot of snakes out there. But they didn't care. Liz kept singing, "I'm so excited" (that great dance song made famous by the Pointer Sisters in 1982) and Lynn was just being Lynn. Finally, after what seemed an eternity, we did arrive at the hotel in Sedona. Seeing the red rock formations for the first time, I was in awe. There was no question that this was an amazing place.

It was soon evident that each of us had ideas as to what we wanted to experience on this trip and that was certainly fine with me. Some of our group wanted to hike the many trails that were spoken of in the guidebooks. Some wanted to enjoy the hotel's spa and others of us hoped to see a number of famous sights, including the Grand Canyon. And so we divided into smaller groups and did just that. Some of the girls spent most of their Sedona time hiking to see all the breathtaking sights and points of interest. Having read all the hiking brochures, Kim and Ginger were their guides. They enjoyed visiting all the red rock formations and shared many laughs along their way. I'm told that our high maintenance Jersey girl Donna feared that they were lost along the trail and spent a good deal of their hike saying "Hail Marys" in the hope of a safe return. Audri on the other hand, loved the hike, but was focused on getting back to town to enjoy a breakfast burrito and a cocktail because it's noon somewhere in the world. Meanwhile, Charlene spent a day of pampering herself at the spa and enjoyed getting beautified.

The remaining seven of us headed north, driving through Flagstaff and across Big Sky country toward the Grand Canyon. Those of us who went to the Grand Canyon were literally brought to tears by the breathtaking magnificence of what we saw. I can't even begin to describe the feeling that swept over us as we looked out onto the huge expanse of canyon. To stand before such amazing beauty was to know God. Each of us felt as though we were on the brink of something far larger than ourselves and sharing that experience is something I will hold in my heart forever.

We all spent time eating in cute little establishments in downtown Sedona and drinking Prickly Pear Margaritas. Some of us drove along old Rte 66 through the quaint cowboy town of Williams, where we bought authentic leather cowboy hats and watched a shoot-'em-up western street show. We visited the new age shops and held crystals in our hands, trying to find the one that was meant especially for us. Six of us even took to the sky, two at a time, flying high above the red rocks in a little

Red Baron biplane! Maggie was so scared, but she went up anyway. With the wind in our faces, she and I flew together, amazed by the wonder of it all!

On our final day, our friends who had done all the hiking suggested that we all go back to a special spot that they had found the day before. As we walked along the flat red rock formations, I was blown away by the beauty. This truly was a magical place! The air was warm and perfectly still as we walked together toward our destination. We knew that we were going to be taking some group photos, so we had all dressed in black shirts and shorts (except for Queen Trudy, who wore white) and most of us donned our new cowboy hats, making us feel quite "Western". When we finally got to the spot, there was a message spelled out with small rocks that said "The Society", left by our hikers the day before to welcome us and any others who might pass by.

Given that the Shaman had told me that I'd come here, it seemed appropriate to take a moment to go off and meditate by myself. There was a place in the rock that jutted out into a narrow ledge. All around it dropped off many feet and it seemed like the perfect spot to have my meditation moment. As I made my way out onto the ledge, I sat cross-legged and closed my eyes in prayer and meditation. I thought of why I was brought there and gave thanks for the opportunity to be sharing this moment with all my friends. Special thanks were offered for the recovery of my friends, Maggie and Trudy, and also for Adam's safe return.

And then, as I sat there in silence, I realized what balance meant. "Balance is found in the breath of contentment." The words came into my head with such clarity and it made perfect sense to me. As we breathe and recognize the wonder of each moment, we find contentment in ourselves. Balance is being content in the present, and only in the present moment can you truly find peace within yourself. I realized that at forty-two years old, I was literally balanced at the mid-point of my life. Half my life was over and the next half was about to begin. While I faced the sadness of "empty nest" and missed the days when my children were little, the next forty-two years were right in front of me! I knew that there would be many new wonderful moments, watching my children succeed as adults, becoming an Auma, retiring with Jake by my side and growing old with my friends. That moment was so profound! And at that moment, a wind greater than any I have ever felt in my entire life surged over me. Out of complete stillness this wind of enormous proportions pierced through my chest and almost literally knocked me backwards off the rock. It was as though an energy force was suddenly there all around me and then, as quickly as it erupted, it disappeared.

When I got off the rock and walked back to my friends, I realized that they all had felt it too, and asked what I had done. It was as though somehow my meditation had brought it to be. We stood in a circle and held hands on the red rocks, knowing that we had just experienced something beyond our comprehension. That day, we reaffirmed our understanding that friendship had gotten us this far and that it would guide us the next part of the journey as well. As I left Sedona, I knew that I would return. The Shaman had been right. Visiting Sedona opened my eyes to see the divine possibilities in us all.

Life is strange in the way that at times we are brought to places along the journey that allow us greater reflection later on. We often don't realize it when we are in the moment, but later, hindsight provides a clearer view of things. In the same way that our visit to New York before 9/11 gave us personal insight into the city and greater appreciation for the catastrophe that followed, the same became true for our visit to New Orleans. I often wondered what became of my Shaman. I pray that he survived the flooding. Perhaps he relocated to Sedona.

August 31, 2005

Today is Wednesday the 31st. . . two days after Hurricane Katrina hit and devastated New Orleans, the Mississippi coast and parts of Alabama. I sit here, from the comfort of my home in my bed, with my morning cup of coffee and I'm speechless as I watch CNN! How horrific for the people trapped in New Orleans with the water rising around them. Without power, clean water or supplies, and with the contamination of raw sewage everywhere, the inevitability of more deaths and disease is in the forefront of my mind. I look at pictures of the streets we visited and I'm astonished at all the loss. Houses are flooded to their rooftops. 20,000 people are trapped in the Super Dome (without supplies or even working bathrooms). People are looting downtown areas. It's truly the largest scale US natural disaster I've ever witnessed. I'm so sad for the people there and for their city. I loved the architecture, the culture and feeling of the city – so much history was there. I can't believe that all the very streets we walked are probably under water. The reports are unbelievable! Gulfport, Mississippi is demolished – the entire coastline is washed out. We still don't know how many people will be counted among the dead. It's heartbreaking! I just keep crying. President Bush needs to send in help right now! The levees need to be repaired and the people need to be rescued! But where will they all go? It's all so overwhelming! And I've been thinking, in the wake of all that is happening in New Orleans, I wonder if the Red Cross will need social worker volunteers and if they do, I wonder if I could get a month's sabbatical from work to go. I wonder if they'd even take me with only one lung. But I can't just sit back and do nothing, so I will inquire. Meanwhile, all I can do is say prayers. . .

After far too long the people of New Orleans were rescued and sent to other cities in the United States like Houston and San Antonio. I did volunteer with the Red Cross, but given my physical limitation of having one lung, they told me that they wouldn't be able to use me down South. Instead, like many others, I wrote a check to the Red Cross and said fervent prayers for all the people who were affected. Back at home, we gradually settled back into our daily routines.

As our children grew up and left our households, work certainly filled the void. Many of us had kids in college and for some of the Sisters, that meant taking on extra jobs. For a while Lynn taught driver's education for a local driving school, in addition to her job as a fourth grade teacher. She and I also worked after school at a program called "Kids' Club". Audri took on more and more hours as a registered nurse and ended up working as the clinical supervisor for a nursing agency. Charlene continued her photography business, but also took a job as an ed. tech at the high school, and Kim went back to work full-time in accounting for the corporate office of a supermarket chain. Maggie and Dale spent many extra hours at the law firm as paralegals.

For years all our activities had centered on the kids, but suddenly it seemed, even with our jobs, we now had the time to do things just for ourselves. At first it seemed a bit strange to have the opportunity to develop our own hobbies and concentrate on our own interests, but with time, I think we all appreciated this change in our lives. Trudy and Dale were very involved in a choral group and participated in local theater productions. Audri played on a women's adult soccer league. Maggie became a reality TV fanatic and devoted quilter. Donna was all about her little Westie dog. Many of the girls joined Curves for exercise and I took up yoga. We started a Society of Sisters book club in which we exchanged recommended readings and we all sought personal reflection in one way or another. Middle age seems to encourage introspection.

My work for the special education department had evolved quite a bit over the years. While I began working at only one elementary school, our Autism population had grown significantly over the years, and now my work brought me to the junior and senior high schools as well. I was blessed to be able to follow my students as they transitioned from grade to grade and school to school, and by this time the children with whom I had first begun my work, were now entering high school. I loved working with children on the spectrum. As different as each child was, they all taught me wonderful insight. Each child held such promise and my ten years of experience proved over and over that the interventions that we were able to provide had really made a difference in their lives. While there were certainly days when my work was challenging and I came home with bruises or bite marks to prove it, I always appreciated the opportunity to work in a field that was so rewarding. I loved being able to take kids therapeutic horseback riding, to teach them cooking, or to help them learn how to play games. When going to work each day is something you look forward to, you know that you are in the right career!

September 4, 2005

With back to school just around the corner, I'm reminded that I no longer have school shopping to do. Gone are the days of choosing new backpacks or lunch boxes, new notebooks and sneakers. I miss that a bit. Wow. Empty nest. It comes in waves for me. I'm fine and then it hits me again. Adam is up in Old Town. Granted Elizabeth still lives here, but her days with us are numbered and she is often off with friends anyway. Soon she too will move away. I've struggled with those feelings of loss the past 6 months or so. It's a blessing and also heartache when your babies graduate from high school. I would think myself strange or crazy to be feeling this way if I didn't have my friends confirming that they feel it, too. Lynn has taken it very hard. Raising teens is Hell. Letting them fly and be free is Hell. But it's all part of life's cycle, I suppose. And if you are fortunate enough, you are left with time for yourself – a time to grow and learn more about who you are, separate from the person named Mom who consumed you for twenty years. And if you are lucky, you and your partner won't have totally lost touch by then. The struggle of raising teens sucks the life out of some relationships and sometimes people are left with a spouse who is a virtual stranger after the kids leave. Jake and I are fortunate, I believe. He is a good man who stood by me during so many obstacles. My cancer, Adam's deployment, Elizabeth's chaos. And I was a basket case some of the time. In turn, I stood by him when he lost jobs and struggled with issues of career. We've gone from no money to some money to no money again, and we never let any of it get the best of us. Now, after living together almost ten years, we are settled into a comfort zone. We both have our own things, own interests, etc., but we come back at the end of the day and reconnect. We have each other's company and that is a wonderful thing. Our relationship isn't as intense as it once was, but for people in our 40's we do o.k. He can still stir my soul. We share a life full of memories and we both look forward to growing old together. I certainly don't want to rush things, but I do look forward to my children's weddings and someday being a grandmother. Maybe that is God's way of completing life's circle. As you mourn the loss of your children's childhood, you are led into a phase of acceptance at becoming a grandparent and continuing on in that way. As a grandparent you can still

*have fun and spoil the little ones without the level of energy you
would need as their parent. God knows that at 42, I don't have
that energy anymore. The Sisters and I have decided to use the
name Auma when we are grandmothers. . . "Auma"– for all the
drama and trauma of getting through parenthood. I like it! So
true! I wonder if Jake will be "Grampie". . . He will like being
Grampie. He loves little kids.*

In spite of our busy schedules, the Sisters still
managed to get together and celebrate every chance we
had, because for my group of friends, life had always been
about celebrating. Maggie threw a wonderful "Survivor
Party" one year, and like on the Survivor TV show, we
divided into two teams and competed for the title of sole
Survivor. Maggie loved reality TV and especially that
show, and she was so excited about hosting the event.
Elizabeth and I helped out by shopping for all sorts of
island decorations and team-colored bandannas, called
"buffs", to be used for the competition. We decorated
Maggie's whole house with a jungle theme and Audri's
daughter, Kayla, painted wonderful "Survivor – Islands of
Insanity" signs to be used as a backdrop. Maggie and her
son, Mike, came up with many challenges for the teams
to play and just like on the show, when a team won a
challenge, the losing team would be faced with voting
off a team member. Complete with a video interview
during the voting process, each contestant had to write
the name of person they were voting off on a little card
and put it in the jar. Then Mike, as host, read the results
to the group. Playing that type of game with a group of
drunken, competitive people sure made for an interesting
and entertaining evening! It was a fun, albeit intense at
times, party that lasted for hours until finally Maggie's
husband, Tom, won the Sole Survivor title. Jake actually
came in second! Maggie's Survivor Party was certainly
another moment in S.O.S. history.

June 26, 2006

*We just got back our annual pilgrimage to North Conway –
most all of us were there – all except Audri. She had to work this
weekend and we really missed her. This year Donna arranged
for us to rent this fabulous house with lots of bedrooms and
bathrooms, a hot tub, and even foosball, air hockey and pool
tables. Over all the years that we've gone to North Conway, one
thing remains the same. Our weekend together is still our yearly
sanctuary. Of course, we've mellowed a bunch over time. Gone
are the days when going out dancing and dressing up took top
billing. We traded in our high heels and bartender cocktails for
comfy pajama pants and homemade blender drinks. It used
to be that we all spent so much time at home that we couldn't
wait to go out, but now, we all spend so much time out at work
that we can't wait to stay in. Over icy glasses of margaritas
and hot tub soaks, we reminisced over all our favorite "remember
when" stories that seem far funnier when told for the hundredth
time. Even some of the girls who had missed out on those early
adventures know the stories so well that they feel like they were
there, too.*

*This year Maggie and I came up with a little plan to stir things
up a bit and add another funny story to our S.O.S. repertoire.
Earlier on in the spring, we both thought that things were getting
incredibly boring and that all the girls needed some perking up.
So, we decided to send everyone a mysterious bottle filled with
S.O.S. inspired items (little Barbies, tiny crowns, and other silly
toys or gadgets) and included in each bottle was a coded message
from someone named "Ms. Teres". Get it? Mystery! God, am I
clever! So, we anonymously sent out the bottles one at a time to
each of our friends and attempted to make it look like our Queen
Charlene was behind the whole thing. The bottles created quite
a stir among the girls and it was fun to hear the email talk pick
up and everyone's energy build. We even created a pseudo email
account and I sent out Ms. Teres emails with cryptic messages to*

our friends. Probably only Maggie and I really deciphered them, but no matter. It was fun. We felt like Nancy-freakin'-Drew.

Given that Maggie and I believe that you can never have too much of a good thing, we decided to use Ms. Teres again in North Conway. Maggie had this whole box of little Barbies that she had bought on eBay (because of course you never know when you might be in need of a little Barbie) and I had this vision of placing all the Barbies on a cake. Like a "welcome to North Conway" cake with a different Barbie representing each of us. But, who would deliver the cake? At first, we thought we'd pay a pizza delivery guy, but we just couldn't get that to work out so that the others would not find out. The next idea was to randomly find someone nearby to make the delivery. On Friday night Maggie and I kept an eye out for any neighbors or people on the street we thought might be willing to make the delivery. Finally when the girls were in the hot tub, we scoped out some biker guy in the yard next door. One thing led to another and Maggie sneaked out to ask the guy if he'd deliver the Barbie cake later that night. It's amazing what people will do when you ask them! Around 9:30 we were all hanging out playing cards and drinking when we thought we heard someone at the door downstairs. When Charlene and Noelle went down to check it out, there, in the doorway, was a Harley Davidson type biker dude holding a Barbie cake! Some of the girls were all freaked out that some random guy opened the door to the house, but Maggie and I thought the whole thing was absolutely hysterical! The more some acted concerned, the more irreverent and impudent we became. As if a biker/stalker carrying a Barbie cake would come to kill a bunch of middle-aged women! There was a Queenly proclamation that Ms. Teres come forward and identify herself, but Maggie and I were sworn to secrecy. After all, our alter egos were Batman and Robin. Didn't they know that a superhero never reveals their identity? Maggie kind of got labeled as the one behind Ms. Teres and certainly it was a joint effort, but truth be told, Ms. Teres was made up by me.

July 5, 2006

This week is such a blessing to me! To have all our family together is something that cannot be taken for granted and I am so grateful to share this time with all of them. Beth and her two girls, Victoria and Marie, have flown in from St. Louis and all the family gathered here yesterday to celebrate the Fourth of July. Both Adam and Elizabeth were here with us and it was a wonderful day of sunshine, swimming, food and sharing. Susan, Allen and their two kids, Austin and Lauren, spent all afternoon with us, and Mom and Dad were here as well. With Beth living in St. Louis, we don't see her or her family as often as we'd like and I miss having the opportunity of watching my nieces grow up. I am so fortunate to have Susan and her two children near by and I appreciate all the time that I spend with them throughout the year. As I watched all the cousins play and splash in the pool together, I was reminded of how important we are to each other. We may live apart from one another. We may be different ages or at separate stages of life and yet we are one. My sisters, all our children and I are blessed with Mom and Dad's love running through our veins. They made us a family and it is because of them that we share facial expressions, body language and use of words . . . little traits that we lose sight of individually but that become obvious when we are together as a group. And those little glimpses of Mom and Dad, along with their loving devotion to us all, will live on. My family feeds my soul and my friends feed my spirit.

With most of our ages spanning mid-life, many of the Sisters had entered the endearing age of menopause. That being said, everything seemed to get on our nerves. Our kids bugged us, our husbands bugged us and we bugged each other. None of us meant to be bitchy and emotional, but as much as we tried not to be, hormones took over. Occasionally even the most gentle of us turned into outspoken crabs. Basically we all felt as though we were going a little insane at times. But like every other stage of our lives, the ones who went through it first were able to guide those who came after them. We knew all about the periods that would last a month followed by nothing but bloating for six months. Cramps and irritability were expected. And we all knew to dress in layers because vicious hot flashes could come upon us out of the blue. We weren't shocked when our bodies weren't working like they were supposed to anymore and our sex lives needed pharmaceutical help to do the things we'd always been able to do naturally. And when we just needed a good cry, we always had each other's shoulders to lean on.

August 19, 2006

My friends continue to be such a lifeline for me. I love them in all their craziness. We've shared some amazing times and trips and pulled together in times of crisis. In spite of all our differences, our group works well together. I often wonder how we are able to maintain our friendship in spite of so many strong personalities? And yet, maybe, that is why our group works so well. There is a synergy that occurs when we are together. Each of us lends her energy to a group dynamic that holds power far greater than any one of us could possibly generate individually. It's bigger than we are.

As in any group, some people become leaders and others followers. I don't profess to be the Society's leader, but I am the planner. When I plan an event or trip, they all come. When we were in New Orleans and even more so when we were in Arizona, I felt that somehow I was a medium for each of my friends. Not in the "tell the future" sort of way, but more as if I was used to open doors for them. Personal doors of experience and reflection, each person in a different way. And I confirm my thinking this way by removing myself from the S.O.S. equation. Without me, had I died, there would be no handbook, no high counsel, no trips to far off cities. Things would now be different for each of them and I smile to think that perhaps I've made some small, zany, nonsensical impact on thirteen women.

Trudy's daughter, Therese, was the first of the Peons to marry, but once the weddings started, it seemed that year after year all the others followed suit. The Sisters came up with the idea that before each Peon wedding, we would celebrate the mother of the bride or groom with something we called the "DAM" (Day About Mom) party, and we also decided that we all definitely needed to own a flask. With all the weddings, showers and celebrations coming our way, it seemed a flask was a welcome accessory to allow us to take up a S.O.S. toast whenever we saw fit. DAM parties were a way to commemorate all the work that the mom had done to get her child to this point in their life. Trudy's party was an evening of pampering – complete with paraffin hand dips, manicures, facials, lots of food, and martini tasting. In the Society's world, every life passage was a reason to celebrate and as moms, we had all worked "DAM" hard to get to that point.

Therese's wedding was held in mid-September at a seaside inn and all the Sisters and their husbands were there. When I think back to that first wedding, I can picture Trudy as mother of the bride. She was so happy and proud. Her rose colored dress with matching jacket was embossed with dainty beige flowers and suited her perfectly. I can not recall a time when she looked more radiant. Trudy had overcome her breast cancer to be present on that special day. As she danced with her husband, Matt, I couldn't help but cry. We were all entering a new phase in our lives and I knew that it would soon be my children who were getting married. Watching Therese and her new husband as they cut their cake, I couldn't help flashing back to those days long ago when eight-year-old Therese would make mud pies on the beach at Drakes Island. Where did all those years go? And yet, with all those years behind us, here we were, the Society of Sisters, together still. Every important moment that I could think of in my adult life included the friends that I cherished. What an amazing gift we'd all been given!

January 11, 2007

I love crawling into bed after Jake's been lying on my side. Sometimes he does that for me in the winter months and it's such a gift. He is better than an electric blanket – such warmth! I can't imagine always being that warm! And he shares it with me! I love that! The sheets and blankets are all toasty. Snuggled here with the icy rain pitter-pattering on the roof, I sip my hot chocolate and smile. It's a good end to a hectic day. Jake is asleep or almost. The rhythm of his breath, offset by the rain. The occasional creak that comes from the radiator or the house itself reaching out to her inhabitants and whispering good night. Our dog Sash moves about getting comfortable downstairs and in time our cats, Max and Charlie, may make their way upstairs. Elizabeth is out and often it's this way. Jake and I, here by ourselves. Settled into bed on a cold winter evening, reading for a little while or writing a few words before lights out. There is comfort in the simplicity of it all. The house is not a mansion, just a home. It is all we need and more and I am truly content here. Jake and I are content with each other, too. We go out now and then to dinner or a movie or maybe the theater. But mostly we live the routine. It's a nice routine though. A comfortable routine. We pay our bills. We make ends meet. We eat well – not extravagantly, but well. We are "pork chop, potpie, and meatball" type of people. Our cars are ten years old, but they are paid for. We don't spend just to spend, but we have plenty. So much to be thankful for. We have won the emotional lottery. We are rich far beyond the limited financial definition of the term – rich in friendship and rich in love.

Chapter Eight
Becoming Auma

July 30, 2010

I wonder sometimes what lies ahead, but I'm thankful that my pages are still blank. Knowing ahead of time would be difficult. I have no doubt that I will have many, many more ups and downs. People I love will die and others may become ill. It's inevitable. People will marry and have babies and perhaps divorce and that too is inevitable. But along the way will be joyous moments and glorious days such as this, when a cup of coffee, an anisette toast cookie and a tranquil garden make me smile. And that is what it's all about. One day, one breath at a time.

As the years passed, the girls and I continued to get together for our monthly Bunko games, but our get-togethers became less and less about the game. Truthfully, after literally playing Bunko every month for seventeen years, no one really cared who won or lost anymore. No one needed any more little trinkets to clutter up our already filled homes. Gift certificates or cash were welcome substitutes. And having played for all those years, it would certainly seem that we all should have known the rules, inside and out. Given our ages, however, and the CRS (Can't Remember Shit) Syndrome that we all suffered from, we often needed to be reminded which table to go to when we won a round and which prizes were for the biggest winner and biggest loser. It was pathetic. God knows the rules had been the same since day one, and we'd all played the game hundreds of times, but some of us joked that we were probably in the beginning stages of Alzheimer's given our mental limitations. It really was quite ridiculous. But as much as we became a bit apathetic about the game, it was hard to give up Bunko all together. Playing Bunko was kind of an institution and certainly part of the S.O.S. culture. It was the one thing that we counted on to bring us together each month. With busy schedules, it becomes harder and harder to plan time together with one friend, let alone ten, and so without our Bunko games, we might have gradually gone our own separate ways.

April 9, 2007

I'm not quite sure why, but I have this wonderful feeling that 2007 is a year of promise. All that I hold dear, my hopes and dreams, are coming to fruition. I have begun my private practice work doing psychotherapy two afternoons and evenings a week and I'm thoroughly enjoying this change. Maybe someday when I'm ready to retire from school, I can do this work a few days a week and have more time to enjoy my retirement years. I'm writing more and that too has purpose. Embracing the idea of mindfulness in every aspect of my life has helped me keep my focus and gives me the courage to walk through doors of opportunity as they open for me. Each day, under the watchful eyes of those I love, I feel empowered to continue the journey. I give thanks for my very best friends.

With winter behind us, I am reminded of the line by Oliver Herford . "We are nearer to Spring then we were in September. . ." I'm encouraged by the promise of warmth and new beginnings found in the blossom of April, but perhaps September holds promise, too. I look forward to this story unfolding one day at a time.

Most of our adult children had moved on with their lives by this time. Some were still away at college and others had moved out of state. I was one of the lucky ones to have my children still somewhat near. Adam was finishing up his last semester at UMO and already had a construction job lined up. Following graduation, he was going to be a construction manager for a company out of the Portland area where he had worked the summer before. Adam was dating a lovely girl named Megan who appreciated his quiet, sincere way of looking at life and seemed to love him for who he was. He had been quite seriously involved a couple of times previously, but in both cases the girls had wanted to change him and, as I had learned long ago, there really is no changing people. You have to love people for who they are. In the end it was a blessing that they had parted ways. Megan was a sweetie, though, and I was very hopeful that following graduation Adam might give her a ring, as I knew that he wanted to settle down.

Meanwhile, Elizabeth was working in an upscale salon on the seacoast, specializing in color. She really enjoyed her work and it was great to see her find both joy and success in her career. I was so proud of her and it was wonderful seeing her so happy. By this time, Elizabeth had been living with her boyfriend John for about a year, and it was no surprise when they came home one Saturday to tell us their big news. They were engaged! Hoping to be married sometime the following summer, they and we had some serious wedding planing to begin!

July 12, 2009

What an amazing day yesterday was! We couldn't have asked for it to be more perfect! The day began with beauty for all! With Elizabeth's friends all being stylists, we spent all morning having our hair and nails done at her shop. It was so much fun! By mid-afternoon we were preparing for the sunset wedding ceremony — Elizabeth had always wanted to get married in the evening. As the sun set, warm orange light filtered in through the stained glass windows of the beautiful little chapel. Floral garland draped each pew along the center aisle and soft white petals laid a romantic path to the altar. As Elizabeth walked down the aisle on the arms of both her fathers, Jake on one side and Chris on the other, I stood at the front of the church watching my beautiful baby girl begin her new life. I was so proud of her and all her accomplishments. With tears of joy, I thanked God for allowing me to be here this day. What a blessing it was to share Elizabeth's wedding day.

Elizabeth looked like a princess! Her strapless white gown had delicate beading across the bodice and a fitted straight skirt that had more of the same beading at the hem. It truly fit her to perfection. A long detachable train trailed behind her in a flutter of lace and beading and on her head she wore an elegant veil. Elizabeth chose Elaine to be her maid of honor, Megan was a bridesmaid and Adam was one of John's ushers. As I listened to the beautiful music and the reciting of vows, I said a silent prayer for their happiness always.

As evening turned to night we left the chapel for the beautiful inn overlooking the ocean. It was a lovely starry night – not too humid, with a light sea breeze, but close to eighty degrees and we couldn't have asked for a better backdrop to this special day. We all had a fabulous time at the reception! Finally, with all the planning behind us, we really were able to kick back, dance, enjoy the amazing food and mingle with all our guests. All of our family were there – my side, Jake's side, and even many of Chris' family attended. I do wish that Chris' father had lived long enough to be a part of Elizabeth's special day, but I know in my heart that he was with us in spirit. What a blessing it was that Mom and Dad were able to attend! Jake and I were thrilled that everything came together so well! I loved being mother of the bride and I must say, I looked quite fabulous myself. I was so thrilled to have found my iceblue dress at the bridal shop in town. Not only did it make me look thin, but it also really brought out the color of my eyes. Of course, the Sisters were there, too – just wouldn't be a party without them. What a fabulous day!

The kids are off on their honeymoon to the Caribbean. They flew out this morning and will cruise from Miami to St. John and three other islands this week. I'm so happy for them. With the wedding over now, Jake and I are taking today to lounge by the pool and reflect on what a wonderful day yesterday really was. I can't wait to see the pictures!

As our children married and started their families, life's never-ending cycle brought my friends and me to where we were once again faced with becoming caregivers. This time, however, we were caring for those special people who had long ago cared for us. With moms and dads who were aging, each of the Sisters began to experience life's role reversal. Many of the girls' parents lived out of state, and they were faced with the difficulties of trying to take an active role in caring for their parents from afar. Traveling to other states and making complicated phone arrangements with area agencies took up much of their time. They faced having parents come live with them or placing them in assisted living housing, but sometimes, in spite of their best intentions, parents did not want their children's help. They wanted to stay in their own homes, even when realistically it was no longer a safe choice. As I watched my friends go through this heart-wrenching process, I dreaded the day when I would be faced with such a situation. I hoped that one day, if necessary, my parents would be able to move closer to me so that Jake and I could be there to help them. Or perhaps they would even live with me, but time would tell. I knew that, like my friend's parents, they would not want to leave their home and I certainly didn't blame them.

One by one, my friends who were about a decade older than I began the cycle. Moms got Alzheimer's and cancer, Dads got cancer and heart disease. Every year, it seemed, someone's parent or in-law died and this left all of us feeling so vulnerable. Whether you are five or fifty, as long as you have your parent alive, you are still someone's little girl. And when finally the day comes that your parents are no longer here, you are left with a great hole in your heart and a void that is only filled by the memories you possess. As we mourned the loss of our parents, each of us relied on our friends to help us find our happiness again. My aunt once shared a saying with me, which speaks to the circumstance of parents aging. It says, "Children, treat your parents tenderly, for the world will be a far less gentle place when they are gone."

With so many difficult things on our plates, the girls and I did not do much traveling in those years except for the occasional weekend away in North Conway. It got harder and harder to plan trips for the whole group. Getting more than ten women to do anything together had been challenging when we were young and easygoing, but getting our group to do so as we entered our fifties and sixties seemed almost impossible. With menopausal hormones still raging for some, I'm afraid at times we were not as tolerant as we once had been. Having friends while in the throes of menopause is much like listening to your favorite song on the loudest volume. It's still your favorite song, but after a while, it still gets on your nerves. Then, when the volume goes back to normal, the song, (and life in general) seems more melodious. None the less, we all knew that this was just part of "the change." I think we all silently prayed that we would still love each other when we were done "changing".

We juggled elderly parents and the births of grandchildren, but first and foremost we were still always moms. No matter how old our own children became, we were there to pick them up or cheer them on. So as we held the emotional aspects of our families together, we plugged along, paying for college tuitions and weddings while trying our best to prepare for retirement.

June 11, 2010

Occasionally, if you are lucky, you are reminded that your work has made a difference in the lives of others. Today was one of those days. This evening, as I sat in the Memorial Gym watching the high school graduates march down the aisle to "Pomp and Circumstance", I looked out into the sea of red and white to find three very special students. These were my students with Autism. They were the kids that I had begun working with my first year as a Phillipstown social worker. Over the twelve years of their education, these students had touched my heart and taught me to see the world through their eyes. Honestly, I wouldn't be in this work if it weren't for them. Knowing them, learning to appreciate who they were and what they were about, made me love the field of Autism. When I think back to their early beginnings, I often wondered how their education would turn out and how they would fare in the world. But this evening, as they sat with their peers, I no longer saw students with special needs, but rather special students. As the evening ended and

I hugged each of my graduates, wishing them congratulations, they told me that they would miss me and they thanked me for being their friend. But it is I who should thank them. I have been blessed to know them.

The Sisters would often joke that the whole gang of us should retire together someplace warm. While that would have been nice, I knew that most of my friends would never really follow through with it. Jake and I had spoken often of retiring in Arizona and early on, we had made that our goal. As we paid off our mortgage and my graduate school loans, we took the money that we had been paying out and invested in a condo in Sedona. Retirement had seemed like a lifetime away, and yet here I was on its doorstep.

With the help of my friend, Ginger, who was a successful real estate broker in Arizona, we were able to find the perfect retirement property. Jake and I wanted a small place with a single car garage that we would be able to use during the winter months once we retired. Our plan was to become "snow birds" (although I always hated that term because I had always heard it used to refer to people far older then I). We would live in Maine May through December because we loved our Maine summers and we wanted to be near the kids through the holidays, but then would head west from January through April. While Arizona is not tropical in the winter, it is certainly more temperate than Maine, and the dry atmosphere was very conducive to better breathing. As I got older, extreme cold or extreme humidity began to bother me more than it had in my youth and my breathing was labored because of it.

We found a perfect little one-bedroom southwestern style condo right in the heart of my amazing red rocks. It was so exciting to think that our dream was becoming a reality. I loved it out west and couldn't wait to retire in a cowboy hat! Jake and I both felt so at home there. Ginger helped us rent out the condo during the months that we lived in Maine and we were so thankful that this worked out as we had hoped. The Shaman was right again. Sedona continued to hold a special place in my heart.

August 25, 2011

What a glorious day! It is sunny and warm – probably close to 80 degrees. As I sit here in our back yard overlooking the pool and the garden, I again feel as though this is my sanctuary. My place of peace. Good karma flags welcome people into this place and green vines grow up along the fence walls. I see Daddy here in the flowers he planted and in the little garden sculpture of children that he gave me. I read words that I painted on the garage wall that make me smile. "Balance is found in the breath of contentment." This garden, this house, makes me smile.

It's not a big home or a fancy home, but its walls have provided for us. They've kept us warm and dry and held secrets of tears and laughter through the years. This October we'll have lived here 15 years. On the front porch, you can sit and rock and look beyond the draping, overgrown wisteria vine with its beautiful purple flowers that bloom in June and imagine yourself in a quaint cottage or seaside home. The sounds of Phillipstown bring you back, however, but that, too, is a pleasant diversion. The cars pass, an occasional truck goes by awakening your senses. Children play and dogs bark. Leaves rustle on the trees making you aware that fall is around the corner. It's a good house. A loving home. The living room with its maroon wallpaper makes me think of years ago and what the "parlor" might have looked like back in the 40's. I have no urge to change things or redecorate as I did in my earlier life, and that tells me I've finally found contentment. It's a cozy house with tin ceilings, a built-in bookshelf, wainscoting throughout and a slope to the ceilings upstairs. It's a cape by style, but more of a bungalow by feel. I love this house and I am truly happy here.

More and more wedding invitations were sent out and the Sisters spent many years in almost constant celebration. In the fall of 2010, Adam and Megan were wed in a beautiful outdoor ceremony under a flower-covered trellis in Megan's family's garden. The final warm breezes of Indian summer lasted just long enough to celebrate with us. A huge tent decorated with thousands of twinkling lights and autumn bouquets provided the perfect ambiance for this unpretentious reception. It suited Adam and Megan perfectly. Chris, who was a justice of the peace, married them in a simple ceremony and, as mother of the groom, I cried as I watched Adam say, "I do." My boy was all grown up. He and I had always had a special relationship. As we danced our mother/son dance, I held on to his broad shoulders and looked into his eyes. For a moment I was back in time to when my little five-year-old boy stood on my shoes as we twirled across the linoleum floor. In my heart, I held that memory of my little boy as I smiled with pride for the man that he'd become. Megan and he were perfect together and I was very happy to know that he had found the right someone to love.

Trudy was the first to become a grandmother. We were all so excited to learn that Therese was expecting and all the Sisters took part in a huge baby shower for her. It was great fun to be buying little baby items again! With this new phase of our lives opening up, we really seemed to be coming full circle. The girls and I had all met during the years when our own children were babies and here we were, a generation later, celebrating the arrival of grandchildren! What a wonderful blessing to be grandmothers together. Therese gave birth to a beautiful baby boy and so it all began again. We laughed to ourselves as our children, once the spirited little people who had kept us hopping, had children of their own and the "mother's curse" of giving birth to children just like themselves was cast in stone. But to the Aumas, all the grandbabies were "angels" and their mischievous energy was precious.

On August 17, 2012 it was my turn to join the other Sisters and become a grandmother. My own precious Emma was born! Elizabeth and John had a baby girl – 8 lbs. 2 oz. and 21 inches long! How I remember that day! Elizabeth had wanted me in the delivery room with her. John was there as her coach, of course, but I was there to hold her hand and lend moral support. I had never delivered naturally myself and, although years ago I had been there with my sister Susan when she delivered my niece and then my nephew, it seemed far more intense now watching my own child. I knew that Elizabeth was scared and I wished that I could take some of her pain, but I was so proud of her. She was amazing! John stayed by her side and encouraged her to give that final push. In those last moments as breathing kept her focused and she squeezed my hand, I saw my beautiful granddaughter for the first time. What a miracle it was to share in life's most amazing moment. I was finally Auma!

After anxiously awaiting the big news, Jake, Chris and John's parents all came in to meet their new little granddaughter for the first time. Adam and Megan also came to welcome our newest family member, as well as my parents, my sister Susan, her daughter Lauren and son Austin. My sister Beth was still living out of state and sent a beautiful flower arrangement. Pink flowers lined the windowsill and a banner on the door read "It's a girl!" Maggie, Lynn, Trudy and Audri all stopped by with gifts and balloons. Elizabeth's best friend Elaine was there, too. What a wonderful day of celebration it was!

When it was my turn to hold Emma for the first time, I cradled this perfect little person in my arms and looked into those precious deep brown eyes. Rocking her gently back and forth in the age-old motion that mothers know by heart, I wondered how it was that love for a grandchild could feel so profound. I felt like my heart was literally bursting with joy! She was a part of me. Life's connections create a legacy and in the end it all comes full circle, creating perfect balance. We are a continuation of each other.

❧

"Well Emma, my dear, this seems as good a spot as any to take a rest. You were born, and the rest, as they say, is history," Auma said jokingly as she got up from the couch. Emma and her grandmother had been sitting together for the better part of four hours sharing the stories. "It's past lunchtime and Grampie Jake is probably hungry. I'm going to make some sandwiches. Would you like to join us?" she asked. Emma declined as she had a few things to do that afternoon at home, but followed Auma back into the kitchen to plan another day that they might get together. At eighty-four, Auma's calendar was still quite full. Wednesday afternoon – Lynn; Friday evening – dinner at Adam's; Saturday morning – grocery shop with Elizabeth; Sunday morning – church meeting. As Auma prepared turkey sandwiches, Emma asked, "Auma, is that your S.O.S. friend, Lynn, that's listed on the calendar?"

"Oh, yes," Auma said with a smile. "She still lives here in town and we try and get together for a cup of coffee every couple of weeks. Neither of us drives anymore, so we have to have someone give us a ride, but yes, we still see each other…and we still make our cinnamon rolls."

"Auma, what ever happened with the time capsule? Did you ever open it?" Emma inquired.

"Yes, yes, we opened it… let's see…of course, I remember. It was New Year's Day of 2025. I was young back then. Only 62. If only I still had the energy that I had at that age! We gathered that evening at Charlene's house because that was where it had been stored all that time. Since it was the "silver anniversary" of our time capsule, we went with a silver theme for the event and bought special silver plated goblets to toast to another twenty-five years! 'Society of Sisters forever!' we cheered! I brought our photo albums and the S.O.S. handbook, and everyone brought any momentos that they had saved.

After our toast, all the girls gathered around our time capsule. One by one, we took each item out of the box. My word! We'd forgotten what all we'd had in there! There was a Phillipstown Gazette dated January 1, 2000 and Lynn's old gray sweatpants! There was a book filled with emails from the time when I was sick and our old Mothers' Club Banner. It was faded but the appliqued letters were all still intact. We laughed as we sorted through our treasures and reminisced over all the old pictures. Before it was time to go, we held hands as we stood in a circle around our capsule. One by one, we looked to the person next to us and named one favorite thing about our friend. As we went around the circle, we stopped at the last person, knowing that the circle was not really complete. Donna had moved out west to live near her son and we missed the energy that she brought to every gathering. It just wasn't the same without her boisterous laugh and we missed hearing her favorite expression, 'That was so enjoyable!' We thought of making a new time capsule, but we didn't really think we'd make it another twenty five years!" Auma said with a wink.

"I keep thinking about all that we've read and the stories you've shared," Emma said. "I've known my whole life how important family is to you, but I never realized just what the Society of Sisters meant to you. I mean, I knew about some of the girls, and my mom has certainly spoken of Lynn and Maggie over the years, but this...this Sisterhood, is something far bigger."

Auma went over to a picture that hung on the kitchen wall and took it down to hold in her hands. She dusted it off with her sleeve. It was a snapshot taken on New Years Eve 2000 – the year of the Society's "Party of the Century". The Sisters, their husbands, and all the Peons, dressed in all their finery, crowded into the shot and smiled widely at the camera. As Auma's finger traced along the faces, Emma noticed tears in her grandmother's eyes.

"I have been incredibly blessed in this life, Emma. That is true. My family has always been there to support me and I have lived my life – all eighty-four years of it – surrounded by their love and warmth. My mother was an inspiration to me. Mom listened to every story I shared, answered every question I asked of her, and taught me the beauty in being able to laugh at myself. She was the most unselfish person I have ever known and it was her example that I held up in my own attempt to be the best mom. From my father, I learned to have faith. Daddy was my mentor. I lived my whole life trying to live up to his expectation and make him proud. My sister Susan taught me to believe in myself and was the keeper of all my childhood memories. My sister Beth surrounded me with loving hugs and the knowledge that, no matter what happened in life, she always cared. My friends, however, were the people who kept me young.

As you know, my life has not been without ups and downs, but no life is. Over the years my friends have all had their share of trials, too, but there is one thing about my friends that makes them different. Most people, when life hands them lemons, do their best to make lemonade. But the Society of Sisters would take the same lemons, trade them in for limes, make margaritas and throw a party!" Auma chuckled at the truth in her words. "Emma, I hope that in your lifetime you hold fast to the women you call friends…they will share all the moments that matter and remind you that no matter how old you become, you can always be a girl at heart."

With that, Auma handed the picture to Emma. "I want you to have this as a reminder of all we've shared. And let's look at that calendar – how does a week from Sunday sound? Come in the afternoon and then we'll have dinner together." Auma suggested. "Grampie Jake would love to spend some time with Glenn while you and I finish the final journal. I think we've read all but one."

⚭

Chapter Nine
Forever Auma

August 17, 2047

    As I sit here in my rocking chair sipping my morning cup of coffee, I feel so blessed to enjoy this day. The sun is shining, the birds are chirping and a warm breeze blows across the porch as I write. What a marvelous day to be alive! Every day should be enjoyed in this way! Today is Emma's 35th birthday and I've been thinking about something special that I'd like to share with her this year. When Elizabeth gave me this book for my birthday a few months ago, I was reminded of how much I used to write. So I dug through my closet to find all my old journals. It seems that I might be missing a few, but it's hard to remember. Years ago I was so good at writing down my thoughts and, reading through a few of them, I've decided to give them to Emma. Perhaps she will appreciate getting to know her grandmother a bit better. This is such a hard time for her, with her divorce from Nick and trying to take care of Glenn. I can remember a time in my own life when I felt that way and maybe knowing that will give her a new understanding of things. Life's journey has its ups and downs, but ultimately it is up to us to make the most of every moment and learn along the way. I look back myself and thank God for all of it. It really has been a wonderful life.

Settling in with a steaming cup of hot cocoa, Emma sat cross-legged on the floor of her bedroom. Spread out across the carpet were her grandmother's old books and scrapbooks. Just six weeks ago Emma had celebrated her thirty-fifth birthday. So much has happened since then… Emma had been given the most wonderful gift! Not only did she have the chance to read Auma's journals, but she had also spent two full days listening to her stories firsthand. What a blessing it had been to have had that special time with her grandmother!

As she glanced toward the kitchen Emma noticed her calendar hanging on the wall. Sunday, October 6th. How ironic to see the name "Auma" marked on this date. Emma realized this was the day that she would have gone to Auma's for dinner to finish hearing her story. So the final chapter of Auma's story was now left to the remaining journal and Emma's imagination. As she ran her hand across the crisp newer pages, Emma noticed that the handwriting appeared shakier than it had in the past. The linear penmanship looked familiar, but it was evident that the scribe was older now than before. There were very few entries left to be read. Perhaps Auma had said all there was to say. Maybe that was why she had taken her leave when she did. She had finished what she intended to do and had left Emma with the secret to a happy life. Growing old was not what mattered - loving life and sharing friendships was.

April 12, 2047

Elizabeth gave me this new book for my birthday. What a lovely dinner we had at her house – all the kids and grandkids were there and they got me my favorite – an ice cream cake! Having family to share your life with is such a blessing!

If there was ever a year to keep a journal, I suppose that this is it. I haven't kept one in many years and yet when I was younger, I wrote all the time. I can't believe that I'm 84. I don't really feel that old, but when I look in the mirror, my reflection tells me otherwise. Happy Birthday to me! Each birthday is a blessing. Sometimes I've wondered if I would ever actually live this long. Years ago I questioned whether I'd make it to 45, and yet here I am. It's a wonderful thing to look back on your life and realize that you have no regrets. You've lived your life to its fullest and, no matter what comes next, you know that it's all o.k. To live that way - no matter what your age - is really the key. Some people seem to spend too much of their time looking forward to tomorrow or dwelling on the past and they never really appreciate the beauty of today. I feel so blessed to have learned that particular lesson when I was young as it really has made a difference in my life.

I've been spending a little time this evening looking through all the old photo albums and scrapbooks. What a life I've had! When I think back to the many wonderful moments with my family and friends, I am so happy to have shared all those memories with them. I have lived long enough to watch my children grow up and have families of their own. I am Auma to 4 grandchildren and Great Auma to 2 great grandchildren! This month Jake and I will celebrate our 50th Wedding anniversary! How time does fly! Somehow, as you get older, the years slip away even more rapidly and all of a sudden you realize that you really are a senior citizen. How did that happen?

While the passage of time has taken many of the people I love, that too is a part of life's process and there is acceptance in it, as well. It's so important to find contentment in whatever the moment presents. I hold the image of my parents in my mind and their spirits in my heart. I thank them both for giving me *support always. I still feel their love with me. I'm blessed to have both my sisters still living. We have shared a lifetime filled with love and laughter. And I think of my friends, the wonderful Society of Sisters, who were always there for me throughout the thick and thin of it, keeping me young at heart. I truly wouldn't have survived motherhood without them. They taught me to laugh in spite of it all. What an amazing gift!*

Two of the Sisters live out of state near their children now, and one has Alzheimer's and is in a nursing home, but seven of the girls have already passed on (as have all but two of their husbands). Sometimes I still have a hard time believing that they are gone. Maybe because they, too, reside within me. We have spent so much time over the past five years attending funerals. It's a strange thing to bury your friends. As I look at the faces of those of us who are left, I know we are all wondering who will be next. Every hug goodbye could be the last, but that is always true for everyone, really. It just becomes more apparent when you get to be our age. At every funeral, we wear our comfort coats of fur even if the weather is too warm for them. It's still just a Society of Sisters thing.

It's a surreal experience to have all the people you love begin to die. I never really gave it much thought when I was younger, but now, I can't help but think about it often. Each life is a celebration of all the moments that you've shared with another. For myself, I'm not afraid to die. I haven't been for a long, long time. I've found balance in my life. I truly believe that we are more than just this body existing in this space and time. If we listen to our hearts, we can find our spiritual selves. We are spiritual beings, experiencing humanity now, and soon we will all be spiritual beings again. Experiencing life is about connecting to people throughout our time here and making memories with them. It's about filling your life with love and friendships. By leaving your story for children and grandchildren, a part of you lives on. You are held in your loved ones' hearts forever.

May 7, 2047

Today would have been Daddy's birthday...

I was looking out at the garden the other day and thinking that he would enjoy seeing how big and beautiful the dogwood tree has become! There are so many memories of him here in my flowers and sometimes when I sit quietly in the backyard, I think I can feel him with me and I know that he is proud. When someone has been gone for a long time, it can be difficult to bring a clear image of him or her to your mind. It's not that you forget, but things get fuzzy. When I think of Dad, I see his gray beard and gentle blue eyes. I have those eyes. He taught me the art of giving and the importance of having faith. I loved being his little girl. I remember standing on Daddy's shoes as he danced me around the kitchen... and he had a wonderful singing voice. Every night, when I was a child, he would sing me to sleep. I would give anything to hear his voice again. Happy Birthday, Daddy!

September 27, 2047

It's getting late but I thought I'd take a moment to write a little bit before bed. What a beautiful day we had today! The sun was shining and there wasn't a cloud in the sky! Jake said it was far too nice to be inside and I had to agree. I've been quite tired lately, but Jake talked me into taking a short walk around the block. As we walked down Main Street, I noticed all the school children scrambling off their busses, excited to be home! What energy children have! As they ran past us into their houses, I thought to myself, "What fun I used to have running and playing with my friends." Remember neighborhood games of Kick the Can and Freeze Tag? We spent hours playing outside and often would stay out until long after dark. I don't notice children playing that way anymore, but that was long before the days of video. What fun they are missing...but perhaps they don't miss what they've never known.

We celebrated Elizabeth's birthday last week. My "baby" turned 61! Where did all that time go? My goodness. . . what a handful she used to be! And yet she grew up to become not only my daughter but also my friend. She's done so well for herself, personally and professionally, and I'm very proud of her. Both my children are wonderful people. A mother couldn't ask for more! I am surrounded by love!

It was a blessing to know that Auma died peacefully as she rested in her garden. She had always said that this was "her" year. Knowing Auma, perhaps she had willed it that way. October 2nd was a good day to go – Sting's birthday, after all. Indian summer days had always been her favorite, days when warm October sunshine mixed with the gentlest of breezes and the smell of "back to school" permeated the air. Surrounded by autumn flowers and serenaded by birds...that was the way she would have wanted to go. Her back yard was her sanctuary and place of peace. After all, it was the place she found balance. She always believed that balance is found in the breath of contentment. And her last breath had been that...filled with contentment.

As Emma put her hand to her heart, she felt a surge of warmth come over her. The energy in the air around her felt electrified and she knew Auma was right there in the room. She understood. We are a continuation of each other and connection is what life's all about. Emma smiled and whispered, "I'll carry you with me always, Auma."

∾

Made in the USA